THE AMERICAN BAR ASSOCIATION

LEGAL GUIDE TO HOME RENOVATION

THE AMERICAN BAR ASSOCIATION

LEGAL GUIDE TO HOME RENOVATION

RANDOM HOUSE REFERENCE
NEW YORK   TORONTO   LONDON   SYDNEY   AUCKLAND

Copyright © 2006 by the American Bar Association

All rights reserved. No part of this book may be reproduced in any form or by any means, electronic or mechanical, including photocopying, recording, or by any information storage and retrieval system, without the written permission of the publisher. Published in the United States by Random House Reference, an imprint of The Random House Information Group, a division of Random House, Inc., New York, and simultaneously in Canada by Random House of Canada Limited, Toronto.

RANDOM HOUSE is a registered trademark of Random House, Inc.

Please address inquiries about electronic licensing of any products for use on a network, in software, or on CD-ROM to the Subsidiary Rights Department, Random House Information Group, fax 212-572-6003.

This book is available at special discounts for bulk purchases for sales promotions or premiums. Special editions, including personalized covers, excerpts of existing books, and corporate imprints, can be created in large quantities for special needs. For more information, write to Random House, Inc., Special Markets/Premium Sales, 1745 Broadway, MD 6-2, New York, NY 10019 or e-mail specialmarkets@randomhouse.com.

Library of Congress Cataloging-in-Publication Data is available.

Visit the Random House Reference Web site: www.randomwords.com

ISBN-13: 978-0-375-72142-7
ISBN-10: 0-375-72142-8

Printed in the United States of America

10 9 8 7 6 5 4 3 2 1

American Bar Association

W. Scott Welch
Baker Donelson
Jackson, Mississippi

David Williams
Vanderbilt University
Law School
Nashville, Tennessee

CONTENTS

Foreword   xi

Introduction   xiii

1 Getting Ready to Renovate: Planning, Financing, and Insurance   1
Save Time and Money by Planning Well

2 Permits, Licenses, and Other Forms of Permission   30
Get it Right, or Pay the Price

3 Do It Yourself   52
From Scheduling to Subcontractors

4 The Contractor   65
How to Choose a Good One

5 Get It in Writing   89
Your Contract with the Contractor

6 The Work   110
Ensuring Your Home Renovation Runs Smoothly

7 Resolving Disputes   133
When Renovations Go Wrong

8 Government Agencies and Legal Protections   158
Some Protection from Unscrupulous Contractors

9 The Role of a Lawyer   172
Finding Help When You Need It

10 Where Do You Go From Here?   186

Appendix   191

Index   203

About the Author   207

FOREWORD

Robert A. Stein,
Executive Director, American Bar Association

When American families are asked to describe their legal needs, the topics that come up repeatedly are personal finance, wills and estates, employment-related law, family and domestic concerns, and various issues related to buying, selling and owning a home. The books in the *American Bar Association Legal Guide* series are designed to address these key legal areas and provide information about the law in plain, direct language.

The goal of this book is to give helpful information on the legal issues that arise when people renovate their homes. This includes coverage of everyday legal issues, including financing renovation, negotiating a contract, resolving disputes, and finding a lawyer. The book explores a range of options that can be used in solving these kinds of legal issues, so that you can make informed decisions on how best to handle your own particular questions. In addition to helping you deal with legal questions that arise during a home renovation, we also hope this book will help you feel more comfortable with the law generally, and will remove much of the mystery from the legal system.

As the largest voluntary professional association in the world and the nation's premier source of legal information, the American Bar Association is in a unique position to provide authoritative guidance on legal issues. The ABA also provides support for lawyer referral programs and pro bono services (where lawyers donate their time), so people like you are able to find the right lawyer and receive quality legal help within their budgets.

This book was written with the aid of ABA members—including lawyers, judges, and academics—from across the country. Their contribution is invaluable because they have experience in dealing with the legal issues that arise in home construction and renovation every day; their perspectives make this a better book.

The ABA's Standing Committee on Public Education provided oversight for this project. The members of this Committee contribute the perspectives of experts in communicating about the law. Public education and public service are two of the most important goals of the American Bar Association. Through publications, outreach, and our website (www.abanet.org), the ABA strives to provide accurate, unbiased legal information to our members, to the media, and to the general public.

Robert A. Stein is the Executive Director of the American Bar Association. He was formerly dean of the University of Minnesota Law School.

INTRODUCTION

Alan S. Kopit, *Chair*
ABA Standing Committee on Public Education

In the last five years, more people have become homeowners than ever before. More people have also become interested in improving their homes, whether they are renovating rooms, adding extensions, or adding a porch or a pool. Some people undertake home improvement projects in order to increase the resale value of their homes; others renovate in order to increase their enjoyment of their homes, or to make room for a new member of the family.

Dozens of television shows deal with aspects of home improvement. These shows often use teams of professionals to create amazing results in just a few weeks, or even a few days. Of course, home improvement is tougher than it looks on television. In the real world, just planning a home improvement and working out the financial aspects can take longer than building a three room extension on a reality TV show.

There are many things you can do to ensure that your home improvement goes smoothly, and protect yourself should things go wrong. If you are working with an architect or a contractor, you will need to enter into contracts with them. You will want to ensure that subcontractors are getting paid and avoid the risk that a subcontractor might place a lien on your home. You should make sure you have insurance that covers people working in your home, your family, and anyone else who might get hurt. If you are making any changes to the structure of your home, you will need a permit. And if a lot of money is involved, you may want to consider buying a performance bond.

This book covers all of these issues, for renovations large and small, in houses, condos, and coops. You will find information on all the legal aspects of home improvement, from planning an improvement, to finding a lawyer if things go wrong.

REVIEWED BY THE EXPERTS

Our principal author is Robert Yates, a lawyer and journalist who has written on a wide range of subjects for the public. He worked with experts on home improvement—including lawyers, architects, and contractors—from all over the country to prepare the final manuscript, with particular assistance from the Construction Forum of the ABA. The entire project was completed under the guidance of the ABA's Standing Committee on Public Education. Together, we've worked to provide you with easy-to-read information that will help you understand and use the law that affects home improvement. Our goal is to help you spot problems before they become major—when they're easiest to handle.

WRITTEN WITH YOU IN MIND

We've made a special effort to make this book practical, by using situations and problems you are likely to encounter. You won't find legal jargon or technicalities here—just concise, straightforward discussions of your options under the law. Each chapter opens with a description of a real-life problem that shows the practical ramifications of the subject. Within chapters, you'll find sidebars with the following icons:

- ▶, which share practical tips that could be of benefit to you;
- ⓘ, which signal key additional information;
- ⚠, which warn you about potential pitfalls that you can navigate with the right information and help;
- 🗏, which give clear, plain English definitions to legal terms;

- **( )** , which highlight experts' responses to practical questions, giving legal information that may help you as you grapple with similar issues that arise when you are renovating your home.

You'll find two additional features at the end of each chapter:

- "The World at Your Fingertips," which contains tips on where to go for more information if you'd like to explore a topic further.
- "Remember This," which highlights the most important points that the chapter has covered.

One word of caution: when reading this book, and other books in the series, keep in mind that these books cannot and do not pretend to provide legal advice. Only a lawyer who understands the facts of your particular case can do that. Although every effort has been made to present material that is as up-to-date as possible, laws can and do change. Laws can also vary widely from one jurisdiction to the next. If you are thinking about pursuing legal action, you should consult first with a lawyer; to find one, contact a bar association or lawyer referral service.

With that in mind, this book can help you to make informed decisions about a wide range of problems and options. Armed with the knowledge and insights this book provides, you can be confident that the decisions you make will be in your best interest.

Alan S. Kopit is a legal-affairs commentator who has appeared on national television for more than fifteen years. He is chair of the ABA's Standing Committee on Public Education and is an attorney in private practice with the firm of Hahn Loeser & Parks, LLP, in Cleveland, Ohio.

CHAPTER 1

Getting Ready to Renovate: Planning, Financing, and Insurance

Save Time and Money by Planning Well

Debbie and Jim have lived in their house for eight years. They love the house, but the family room is starting to feel too small for them and their growing children, and Debbie's never been crazy about the kitchen. Rather than look for a new house, they decide to renovate the two rooms, expanding them both and modernizing the kitchen. But before they start calling around for contractors, Debbie and Jim need to do some advance planning.

Debbie and Jim are not the only homeowners thinking about redoing a kitchen, adding a bedroom, or fixing up a bathroom. According to Harvard University's Joint Center for Housing Studies, homeowners spent about $138 billion completing nearly 50 million home renovation projects in 2004. That's a lot of remodeling!

Renovation can be a great way to make your home a more enjoyable place to live while adding to the value of what is, for most people, their most valuable financial asset. To some extent, however, the business of home renovation is fraught with uncertainty. Anyone who has considered renovating a home has heard horror stories about contractors not showing up, or about a job costing twice as much and taking twice as long as was planned.

But it doesn't have to be like that. Instead, you can make the process of renovation much easier by planning carefully and understanding the laws and legal relationships involved.

This book has been written to help you understand how to manage a renovation—to plan it well, select the best contractor you can, negotiate a good contract, and make sure the contractor stays on the ball (and on the job)—so that you can prevent the inevitable problems that arise during construction from becoming full-fledged legal problems. This book will also help you to protect yourself legally when there is no alternative but to call in the lawyers.

This introductory chapter will guide you through the steps you need to take when considering a home renovation—from a cost-benefit analysis of whether renovation is right for you, to dealing with financing and insurance.

THE COSTS AND BENEFITS OF RENOVATION

You've always wanted to convert the bathtub in your downstairs bathroom into a shower—and, while you're at it, replace the toilet and the sink. Or perhaps you're looking to add a new bedroom to accommodate your growing family. Such projects may seem like worthy undertakings, but because you're going to be spending money on any renovation that you make, you need to decide whether it will be worth the cost. All renovation projects are disruptive to your home, both physically and emotionally. They're dusty, they're noisy, and they interfere with your daily routine—from the first smack of the sledgehammer to the final stroke of the paintbrush. And every renovation project is expensive—usually more expensive than you first think it will be. So before you begin, ask yourself: Is it going to be worth it?

The first factor to consider is how much the finished project will add to your enjoyment of your home. Only you have a sense of how much a renovation will enhance your home life—of whether it's an absolute necessity or more of a luxury. Think about how long you plan to stay in your home; the longer you plan to stay, the longer you can enjoy the fruits of your project. If you plan to stay for a long time, you may be able to justify a quirky feature or extravagance that might not be appreciated by another owner. If you expect to move sooner, however, you shouldn't make improvements that could have a poor return when you sell your home.

When deciding whether to renovate, the second factor to consider is potential return on your investment. While it's impossible to put a value on the happiness generated by a renovation, statistics can help us predict the resulting increase in your home's resale value. In terms of cost, the question is whether a proposed renovation will pay for itself through an increase in the resale value of your home. A word of caution, however: The value of your home depends on many factors other than just the improvements made to it. Location, location, location, as well as the overall condition of your home, will have the greatest effect on its value—but renovation will also play its part. Generally speaking, most renovation costs will likely be recovered when you sell your home, as indicated by the following rough statistics:

- If you renovate your kitchen, your home's resale value will likely increase by 90 to 100 percent of the renovation cost. (In other words, you will likely recoup 90 to 100 percent of the cost of renovation.)

- If you add a bathroom to your home, you will likely recoup about 90 percent of the cost when you resell.

- If you add a family room, you will likely recoup about 85 percent of the cost.

- If you renovate a bathroom, you will likely recoup about 75 percent of the cost.

- If you add a deck, you will likely recoup about 75 percent of its cost.

- If you renovate a home office, you will likely recoup about 70 percent of the cost.

Depending on the state in which you live, you may only be able to recoup about half the cost of adding a swimming pool. In states such as California and Florida, swimming pools are expected amenities in higher-end homes, and may not add much value. Swimming pools in northern states, on the other hand, may put off as many buyers as they attract, because they require maintenance and cannot be used year-round.

TALKING TO A LAWYER

Q. A condo I was thinking of buying is marked as a handicap unit by the developer. If I buy it, will I be able to modify it and get rid of the handicap accessibility?

A. If the developer was required to include a certain number of handicap accessible units in the complex, then it is unlikely that you will be able to remove the features that make the unit accessible. Talk to the developer about this issue.

—**Answer by Gerald Niesar, Niesar Curls Bartling LLP, San Francisco, California**

You may wish to talk to a realtor in your area about how renovation may affect the value of your home.

BUDGETING YOUR RENOVATION

Once you've performed an initial cost-benefit analysis and decided that you want to renovate, it's time to figure out how much you can afford to spend. There are numerous ways to finance your home renovation—from home equity loans, to savings, to having your contractor arrange a loan for you. But before you decide on a method of financing, you need to sit down and work through the numbers. Don't hesitate to tap into the expertise of a financial advisor or banker. Even at this preliminary stage, a professional can help you estimate a project's cost to determine whether you really can afford it.

Once you've determined what you can afford, and before you talk to an architect or contractor, resolve to stick to your budget. Plan to spend just 80 percent of the budgeted amount, and set aside the other 20 percent for unforeseen changes and additional costs that are bound to arise.

$12,000 FOR A BATHROOM!

According to a Harvard study, the average do-it-yourself cost of a minor bathroom renovation was $701 in 2004. The average do-it-yourself cost of a major bathroom renovation was $5,186. For those who relied on professionals to do the job, a minor bathroom overhaul cost $1,712, while a major remodeling cost $12,272.

KNOW YOUR LEGAL RIGHTS AND OBLIGATIONS BEFORE YOU START

Once you've given your renovation project a green light, it's a good idea to sit down with a lawyer to discuss the legal issues that will arise as the project gets moving. In a typical home renovation, every involved party has legal responsibilities. You, the homeowner, will owe contractors and subcontractors money in exchange for their work, and could face severe consequences if you fail to pay. You also owe contractors a safe place to work. If an electrician trips over your child's toy and falls down a flight of stairs, you could face legal and financial consequences. In return, contractors owe you a workmanlike job, completed on time, for the agreed-upon amount of money.

A lawyer can give you advice on drafting a contract that best protects your legal interests. Your best bet is to see a specialist— either a real estate or construction lawyer. An experienced lawyer can tell you what steps you must take legally, and can alert you to potential pitfalls and how best to avoid them. Especially if the project is an expensive one, it's a good idea to spend a few hundred dollars at the outset for good legal advice, to avoid spending tens of thousands of dollars later if things go sour. Establish a relationship with your lawyer early in the project, when things are tranquil—before you desperately need his or her services later.

Before you go any further, you should also determine whether you need a building permit. Call your local building department (the name of the department differs from place to place), describe the work you plan to do, and ask if a permit is required. Municipalities vary widely in their requirements—some even require permits for changing electrical outlets—so don't assume anything. If your project includes work on the exterior of your house, you should also check with your local zoning department, as you may need to apply for a variance. Reliable contractors should know what permits are required, but don't take their word for it. As the homeowner, it's *your* responsibility to obtain the required permits—and you'll be the one to suffer the consequences if you don't. Many cities and counties post permit and zoning information on their websites; see the end of this chapter for contact information.

If you live in a condominium, a cooperative apartment, a planned unit development, or other common-interest property, your rights to renovate are likely restricted. Check the deed to your property or the applicable rules or bylaws for any covenants, conditions, or restrictions that limit use of your property. Most homeowners' associations require you to ask permission of a homeowners' board in order to make changes. Again, assume nothing: even small projects, such as changing the height of a fence, may be restricted.

Your right to renovate may also be restricted if you live in a historic district. Check with the local district board, landmarks commission, or architectural-standards compliance committee before starting any project.

CONTRACTOR ESTIMATES

Once you have a good idea of what you want and what you can afford, it's time to start looking for an architect or contractor. It's a good idea to have some estimates from contractors before you seek financing for the project. If you're embarking on a large, complicated project, you should seriously consider using an architect to draw your plans. If the project is fairly straight-forward, however, a good contractor may be sufficient for your needs. Ask at least three contractors to visit your home to discuss the project and see what you have in mind. After the contractors check out the space, they will send you bids. Review the bids thoroughly to make sure they take into account all of the work necessary to complete your project.

If the bids exceed your budget for the project, work with your architect or contractor to modify the construction plans in order to reduce costs. Your options include simplifying the design of your project, eliminating certain features from the finished space, or cutting back on finishing materials—but no matter what, you should stick to your budget. If the project lends itself to phasing or staging, you can complete the work one step at a time, deferring each phase until you can afford it. There might also be elements of the project you can complete yourself in order to get more for less. If it turns out that the renovation of your dreams doesn't fit within your budget, then you'll have to modify your plans—or put the project on hold until you can afford it.

Once you've received a bid within your budget, it's time to look for financing.

FINANCING

By this point, you should have your ducks in a row. You know what your finished renovation will look like, you know what permits and licenses are needed, and you know how much the project will cost. Now you're looking for money. It's at this stage of your project that the potential return on your investment comes into play.

Base your financing decision on how the project is likely to affect your home's estimated resale value. If the project isn't likely to add much value to your home, you'll probably want to take out a short-term loan, or borrow against your retirement fund or life insurance, so that you can pay off the project before

FINANCIAL PLANNING

When it comes to financing, the most common problem of all is running out of money before the project is completed. Running out of money—whether altogether or temporarily—can easily destroy the value of the work completed thus far, and waste all the money already paid to the contractor. The best way to limit this risk is through careful planning. Prepare your budget with the worst-case (most-expensive) scenario in mind for every part of the project, and add at least 20 percent to your total estimated cost. The most important protection against overspending is knowing exactly what your project entails, so that you don't have to make changes during the project.

you sell the home. If you're renovating a kitchen or adding a bathroom, on the other hand, long-term financing may be more appropriate. Long-term financing will allow you to pay off the renovation when you sell the house—provided that you sell before you've finished paying off the loan.

Savings and Investments

The first place to look for money is in your own accounts. Tapping into savings and investment accounts may be more cost-effective than taking out a loan to pay for your project, as the interest rate on most consumer loans will likely be higher than the rate of return on your investments.

Paying Cash

If you have cash available to pay for your remodeling project, this may be the best way to go. You won't carry any debt; when the project is done and paid for, it'll be yours free and clear.

The other side of this coin is that when you pay cash, you tie up money that could be earning interest in other investments. Before you dip into your savings, take a look at the interest rate you would be charged if you used a loan to finance your project. Compare that interest rate to the rate of return you could earn by investing the same amount of money. If the latter is higher than the former, investing may be a better option. In addition, interest payments on a home renovation loan may be tax-deductible, while you can't write off the expenses of a renovation project paid for in cash. Consider also your level of financial discipline. If you are confident that you can and will make the monthly payments on a loan, it might be a good idea to leave your savings alone and borrow the project funds.

Sit down with a financial advisor to determine whether paying for the project in cash will really pay off for you in the long run.

Borrowing against Your Retirement Funds

If you have a 401(k) or 403(b) retirement plan, you may be able to borrow against it to finance your home renovation project. Of all the possible methods of financing, this is probably the simplest. Closing costs, if any, are minimal; it's your money, so there's no credit check; you can access the money quickly; and the rates are low, generally a point or two over prime. An added bonus is that the interest you pay goes back into your retirement fund—so, in essence, you're paying back yourself.

Tapping into your retirement fund works best for smaller projects, because you'll have to pay back the loan in a fairly short time period; if you fail to repay the loan within five years, you'll be subject to heavy penalties and taxes. Also note that if you leave your job after having borrowed from your 401(k), you'll have to pay back the loan in full or face similarly heavy withdrawal penalties and taxes.

Life Insurance Loans

Borrowing against the cash value of your life insurance policy is another simple way to access money. Generally, you can borrow up to 96 percent of the policy's cash value at a low interest rate. The face value of the policy will be reduced by the amount of the loan until you repay, which means that if you die before the loan is repaid, your beneficiaries will receive a smaller payout. As is the case with borrowing from your retirement funds, borrowing against your life insurance policy is a strategy that is most appropriate in the case of smaller projects.

Borrowing from Your Portfolio

Another option for financing your project is to take out a margin loan against your own portfolio of securities. Most brokerage houses cap margin loans at 50 percent of the total value of your securities, but the actual percentage that you can borrow on margin will depend on several factors, including the purpose of the loan and the volatility of the stocks you own. As is always the case when the stock market is involved, a margin loan can be a bit of a gamble. If the market does well, you don't have to pay back the loan. But if the market sinks, the value of your collateral drops—and, if it is no longer enough to secure the loan, you could be forced to sell the stock.

Loans

If you'd rather borrow the money for your project than pay for it yourself, or if financing the project is the only realistic way to get it done, then it's time to talk to lenders.

There are several institutions that can loan you money, and a surprising number of different kinds of loans available—not all of them offered by the traditional banking sources—so shop around before you commit to a loan. You're familiar with banks, savings and loans, and credit unions, but mortgage brokers and specialized lenders are two other types of institutions that can also finance your project.

Mortgage brokers represent a number of money sources, including regional and national banks, specialized lenders, insurance companies, and wealthy individuals. As a result, brokers can offer a wide variety of financing options. Specialized lenders, on the other hand, specialize in one or two specific types of loans. Their strength is that their employees tend to be very knowledgeable about the types of loans they offer. In addition,

WHAT IS YOUR HOME WORTH?

Lenders will not extend you financing unless they know the market value of your existing home. For this reason, a lender typically will appraise your home before making a decision about your application. Most lenders will underwrite a loan that is 80 percent of the appraised or market value of the home, minus your current mortgage loan balance.

 ## HOW MUCH CAN YOU AFFORD?

The debt-to-income ratio is the most common factor considered by lenders when assessing an applicant. It is calculated by dividing the amount of your fixed monthly expenses by the amount of your gross monthly income. As a basic rule, an applicant's debt-to-income ratio should not exceed 36 percent.

For purposes of this calculation, your fixed monthly expenses include:

- Monthly housing expenses (loan payments, taxes, insurance)
- Estimated monthly payments on your home renovation loan
- Monthly revolving–credit line payments (credit cards) and other monthly installment loan payments
- Real estate loan payments on non-income-producing property
- Alimony and child support payments

An applicant's ability to repay a loan is an important factor that lenders consider when qualifying him or her for financing. If lenders think it may be difficult for you to make the necessary payments, you will need to do one of the following in order to qualify: reduce the amount you want to borrow; increase your income; or pay off outstanding debts.

many specialized lenders have streamlined processing to the point where they can offer very competitive rates. Their limitation, however, is that they won't offer you a wide range of financing options.

Interest Rates

The annual percentage rate (APR) is the most important factor to consider when you shop for a loan. An APR reflects the interest rate, mortgage broker fees, points, and other credit charges the lender will require a borrower to pay, and expresses these costs in terms of a single yearly rate. Generally, the lower the APR, the lower the cost of your loan.

In addition, ask your lender about the nature of the rate on your loan. In some cases, the interest rate will remain the same throughout the life of the loan. These loans are known as **fixed rate loans**. With other loans, the applicable interest rate is tied to market conditions. These loans are known as **variable rate loans**. Typically, the rate on variable-rate loans is linked to a market-wide interest rate—such as the prime rate, which is the interest rate that big banks charge their best big-business customers—or some other financial-index number. For example, the interest rate on a variable-rate loan might be set at "prime plus two," which means that the rate on the loan will always be two percentage points higher than the current prime rate. As the prime rate falls, the loan rate drops, and as the prime rate increases, the loan rate rises. Adjustments to the rate are typically made every quarter or every six months.

There are several additional questions you should ask your lender to help you determine the total cost of your loan:

• What points and other fees will you be charged by the lender? Points usually are paid in cash at closing, but may be financed. If you finance points, you'll have to pay additional interest, which will increase the total cost of your loan.

• What is the term of the loan? In other words, how many years will you be required to make payments?

POINTS

Points are fees paid to a lender or broker for a loan, and are often linked to the loan's interest rate. One point usually equals one percent of the loan amount. Normally, the more points you pay to a lender, the lower your interest rate will be. The Federal Trade Commission recommends to consumers that they ask for points to be quoted in terms of a dollar amount, rather than in terms of a number.

SECURED AND UNSECURED LOANS

In a **secured loan**, the borrower makes two promises to the lender: first, the borrower will repay the loan; second, if the borrower does not repay the loan, the lender has the right to take the borrower's property and sell it to pay off the loan. The property promised by the borrower is called the **security**. The security promised in most home renovation projects is the house. If you don't repay a secured loan, you lose your house. But, because a house is a substantial asset, securing a loan with your home means that you are more likely to be able to borrow more money at a lower interest rate. (This is because interest rates are a sign of the lender's risk—the riskier a loan, the higher the rate). One benefit of a secured loan is that the interest is probably tax-deductible.

If a homeowner has enough equity in his or her home, the home can be promised as security for more than one loan. Usually, a mortgage on a house indicates that the homeowner borrowed to buy the house in the first place. If the homeowner uses the house to secure a second loan, the lender for the second loan has a **second mortgage** on the house. What this all means is that if the house has to be sold to pay off a loan, the holder of the first mortgage gets paid first.

In an **unsecured loan**, the borrower agrees to repay the amount of the loan according to a schedule of installment payments, but the lender cannot automatically seize the borrower's property if the borrower fails to repay. (In order to be able to seize the property, the lender would have to sue the borrower and obtain a judgment.) Because unsecured loans are a riskier investment for lenders, they generally have higher interest rates than secured loans, and are usually for shorter terms and smaller amounts than secured loans.

- What will be the total amount of your monthly payment? Will it stay the same or change? Does the payment amount include escrows for taxes and insurance?
- Does the loan include a balloon payment? A **balloon payment** is a large payment usually made at the end of a loan term, often after a borrower has made a series of lower monthly payments. When the balloon payment is due, you *must* come up with the money.
- Are there prepayment penalties? **Prepayment penalties** are extra fees that may be due if you pay off a loan early by refinancing or selling your home. By making it too expensive to get out of loans, prepayment penalties often force borrowers to keep high-rate loans.

Types of Loans

As this section will demonstrate, there are many different types of loans. The type of loan that's right for you will depend on your circumstances.

Home Equity Loans

With a home equity loan, the amount you can borrow is based on the equity you have accumulated in your home. Lenders will typically lend up to 75 percent or 80 percent of a home's equity value. To determine how much equity you have in your home, subtract the unpaid balance of your mortgage from the fair market value of your home.

A home equity loan is secured by your home, so you can write off the interest paid on the loan during the year on your income tax return. Most home equity loans are fixed-rate, five- to twenty-year loans, and the interest rates are slightly higher than those on a standard thirty-year loan. Loan fees can be high: large banks may charge two to five points at closing; brokers and finance companies may charge ten to twenty points. Closing costs may also include appraisal, title search, credit check, and application fees. Be careful: Make sure you can afford the monthly payments before you sign. If you can't make the payments, you may lose your home.

Home Equity Lines of Credit

A home equity line of credit is an open-ended, adjustable-rate line of credit for which your home serves as collateral. The credit line is typically limited to 75 percent to 80 percent of the equity value in your home. Home equity lines of credit usually carry a variable interest rate based on the current prime rate or another index. Because such credit lines are secured by your home, as is the case with home equity loans, the interest paid is tax-deductible. The interest rate is generally about 1.5 percent higher than that on a first mortgage, but is not charged until you actually borrow the money—that is, spend some of the money in the line of credit, which you may do whenever you choose. Closing costs and paperwork are much simpler with home equity lines of credit than with first mortgages. The greatest advantage is that lines of credit can be paid off and used again whenever the borrower chooses. The danger, however, is that it's very easy to go over budget.

Cash-Out Refinancing

If interest rates today are lower by 2 percent or more than when you first bought your home, refinancing your mortgage can be a smart move. Refinancing allows you to use the equity in your home to take out a new loan, pay off your existing mortgage, and then use the remaining funds for your renovation project.

Before you decide to refinance, however, consider how long you plan to live in your home and whether the number of years left on your current mortgage makes refinancing worth your while. A typical refinance involves an adjustable or fixed-rate fifteen- to forty-year loan for 75 percent to 80 percent of the home's appraised value. Depending on the balance of the original mortgage, the remaining cash from the refinancing can be used at the homeowner's discretion. Closing costs may include appraisal and points. And, as with your original mortgage, the interest paid on a refinanced loan is tax-deductible.

To get the best deal, shop around. Some lenders will refinance up to 95 percent of a home's appraised value, though interest rates in such cases will typically be higher.

Value-Added Mortgages

Value-added mortgages are a new way of financing home renovation. With a value-added mortgage, instead of lending you 80 percent of the current value of your home, a lender loans you 80 percent of the value your home will have when the renovations are complete. These mortgages are most appropriate in situations where the improvements you make will have a very substantial impact on the market value of the home. For example, you might be able to get this kind of loan if your home is small or outdated in comparison to the rest of your neighborhood.

The interest rates on value-added mortgages can be comparable to the rates on first mortgages. Funds from the mortgage are usually released in a series of payments called **draws** as certain stages of the project are completed. Fannie Mae's Home-Style Mortgage, discussed in more detail below, is an example of a value-added mortgage.

Home Improvement Loans

The Federal Housing Administration (FHA) of the U.S. Department of Housing and Urban Development insures certain home renovation loans under its Title I and Section 203(k) programs. Under these programs, a borrower obtains a loan from a private lender, but FHA insures repayment of up to 90 percent of the loan. Loans for less than $7,500 do not require a lien against the borrower's property, and FHA loans do not carry prepayment penalties.

A **Title I loan** allows you to borrow up to $25,000 for improvements to a single-family home; no equity is needed for loans under $15,000, and no security is needed in most cases for loans under $7,500. These are fixed-rate loans made by approved Title I lenders that FHA insures against the risk of default, which means that banks and other lenders lend from their own funds, and the Federal Housing Administration insures them. The interest rates are negotiable with the individual lenders, and the loans can't be used to pay for luxury or nonessential improvements such as swimming pools.

A **203(k) loan** is a single, long-term, fixed- or adjustable-rate mortgage that can cover both the purchase and the rehabilitation of a property. A 203(k) loan is generally used to update or improve a house or condominium needing a minimum of $5,000 in essential repairs—for example, new wiring, plumbing, roof repair, or structural repairs. Such a loan can also be a great way to buy a home that needs a lot of work. To obtain a loan under the 203(k) program, you must use an FHA-approved lending institution, which includes most mortgage lenders. The amount of a 203(k) mortgage is based on the projected value of the home after the renovation, so it actually includes the cost of the renovation itself. A portion of the mortgage is used to pay for the purchase of the home, and the remainder is placed in an escrow account for the renovation; funds are released in stages as the renovation proceeds. The down payment can be as little as 3 percent.

HomeStyle Renovation Loans

Fannie Mae offers loans through its HomeStyle Renovation and HomeStyle Remodeling mortgage programs. Unlike the Title I and Section 203(k) loans described above, these loans are not guaranteed.

A **Remodeler loan** is a combination of a mortgage and construction loan. Borrowers must hire licensed contractors and submit work plans for approval by the lender. As the work is completed, the lender is responsible for inspecting the work and paying the contractor. HomeStyle Remodeler loans can't exceed 110 percent of the value of the property after renovation, and the minimum down payment required to obtain the mortgage is 5 percent instead of the 3 percent required for a 203(k) loan.

The Community Reinvestment Act requires financial and lending institutions to meet the credit and banking needs of all the communities in their service areas, including low-income and minority communities. As a result, special funds or loan programs may be available to low- and moderate-income homeowners in certain areas. Contact the Federal Home Loan Bank for information about your area.

Unsecured Loans

An unsecured loan is best when you're dealing with a project under $10,000. You won't incur the costs associated with secured loans, but the interest rate on the loan will be higher. Unsecured loans usually are for a small amount, are issued by a bank, finance company, or credit union, and do not involve a lien on your home. Some form of collateral, such as a savings account, is usually required to obtain an unsecured loan. If you default on the loan, the lender will place a hold on the funds in the savings account or on your other collateral. Unsecured loans are short-term, fixed-rate loans, and the interest paid on them is not tax-deductible.

Consumer Credit

The term **consumer credit** refers to unsecured, high-interest lines of credit with no restrictions on their use. This kind of credit is expensive and should only be used for emergencies—not to pay for a home renovation project. The interest paid on consumer credit is not tax-deductible. Consumer credit agencies, which are also called credit counseling and debt consolidation agencies, are set up to loan money for emergencies and to consolidate debt for people in over their heads. Such agencies represent one option for financing—but, frankly, not a very good one.

Credit Cards

The main advantage of using credit cards or cash advance checks is the ease with which you can initiate a loan: simply use your credit card or write a check. Of course, such loans are unsecured and typically carry high interest rates—often 20 percent or higher. As a result, it's best to think of credit cards the same way you think of consumer credit: as an option for emergency use, but not for home renovation.

Homeowner Loans

Homeowner loans are loans based on your income and secured by your home, for as much as $25,000. If you have a high income but little equity in your home, such loans are a good option. The interest rate is usually 3 percent higher than that on a first mortgage, but the closing costs are lower, because there is no formal appraisal of your home and the paperwork is easier. Moreover, because homeowner loans are secured by your home, the interest paid on them is tax-deductible.

Contractor Financing

Some contractors have relationships with lending institutions through which consumers may obtain financing. In these types of arrangements, a consumer fills out a credit application given to him or her by the contractor. The lending institution then purchases that contract from the contractor by paying the amount charged by the contractor to perform the work. The consumer then repays the lending institution directly through a series of installment payments. In contractor financing arrangements, you can expect to pay interest rates of about 20 percent.

Lien Contracts

Lien contracts involve the placing of a lien or deed of trust against your home or property. This means that if you default, the lender can foreclose on your home and sell it to collect what it is owed. If this happens, the homeowner rarely receives anything from the sale of the home, no matter how small the debt owed.

Never sign a lien contract unless advised to do so by a lawyer, and unless you completely understand all its terms. All lien contracts must contain a statement of the home's full cash price, the amount of the down payment, the amount financed, applicable interest rates and finance charges, the amount and dates of periodic payments, the amount of total payments, and the total deferred payment price. These contracts must also contain a written notice of your right to cancel the contract within three days of signing.

Generally speaking, it is best to stay far away from these loans, even if the terms appear reasonable. Not only is it a bad idea to have a contractor secure your financing, but in some states it may also be illegal. Even if a contractor is willing to approve you as a credit risk when a bank won't, he has a good reason for doing so: his guarantee that you'll pay him back is your home. If this is the only way you can finance the project, don't do it.

Redevelopment Agencies

Many states, cities, and counties offer grants and low-interest loans for low-income homeowners and homeowners in low-income neighborhoods. Such loans and grants are offered through redevelopment agencies, which you can locate using government websites. Because the goal of these agencies is to improve the housing stock in low-income neighborhoods, grants and loans are restricted to those earning beneath a certain income level. If you qualify, you may find yourself eligible for loans at or even below market rates. The loan amounts available and the interest rates will vary from city to city; check with your local agency for more information.

THE LAW ON LENDING

There are two federal laws that regulate aspects of lending: the federal Truth in Lending Act, and the Home Ownership and Equity Protection Act.

AFTER CHOOSING A LENDER

After you've chosen an appropriate loan and lender, you may still want to ask a few important questions:

- It never hurts to ask if the lender will lower your APR, eliminate a charge you don't want to pay, or remove a loan term that you don't like.

- Ask the lender for blank copies of the forms you will sign at closing. (Most legitimate lenders will grant this request.) Take the forms home and review them. If you don't understand them, call an attorney.

- Ask the lender to give you copies of the actual documents after you've signed them.

- If you are refinancing a first mortgage, ask if the loan's monthly payment includes an escrow amount for property taxes and homeowner's insurance. If not, be sure to budget for those amounts.

Truth in Lending Act (TILA)

If you have second thoughts after signing for a loan, the federal Truth in Lending Act (TILA) gives you three business days after closing to cancel the contract. This is called the **right of rescission.**

If TILA applies, which it will in nearly every situation in which a lender obtains a security interest in a borrower's principal residence, the lender must give you at signing two copies of a notice indicating your right of rescission. The notice must be separate from the contract and must identify the transaction, disclose the security interest in your home, inform you of your right to rescind, tell you how to exercise that right, explain the effects of rescission, and inform you of the date on which the rescission period expires.

Under TILA, the lender also must prominently state the annual percentage rate of interest you'll be charged for your loan.

The result is that, whether you finance your home renovation through a bank, a credit union, or the contractor himself, you'll always know the applicable interest rate.

If the lender fails to disclose your right of rescission or the credit terms, the period during which you may exercise the right of rescission automatically extends from three days to three years.

To rescind, you must notify the creditor in writing. Send your letter by certified mail, and request a return receipt. This will allow you to keep track of what documents the lender received and when it received them. Be sure to keep copies of all correspondence with the lender, as well as any enclosures. After you rescind, the lender has twenty days to return the money you paid as part of the credit transaction, and to release any security interest in your home. Remember that you must then return the creditor's money or property, which might mean getting a new loan from another lender.

The Home Ownership and Equity Protection Act (HOEPA)

The Home Ownership and Equity Protection Act (HOEPA), which is a part of the Truth in Lending Act, was designed to protect lower-income borrowers from lenders who charge high rates and high fees. HOEPA prohibits deceptive and unfair lending practices with respect to home equity loans, second mortgages, or refinances secured by a borrower's home. It applies if (1) the loan's APR is more than 8 percent higher (in the case of a first mortgage) or 10 percent higher (in the case of a second mortgage) than the rate on a Treasury note of comparable maturity; or (2) the fees and points at closing total 8 percent or more of the total loan amount. For purposes of determining whether HOEPA applies, credit insurance premiums that are written in connection with the loan count as fees (credit insurance is discussed in more detail on page 26).

If HOEPA applies to your situation, then in addition to the disclosures required under TILA:

1. A lender may not lend based on home equity without regard to your ability to repay the loan;

2. You must get certain disclosures from the lender at least three business days before signing the loan;

3. Your lender cannot make a direct payment to your contractor;

4. Certain loan terms are illegal—such as most prepayment penalties and increased interest rates at default; and

5. Balloon payments for loans due in less than five years are prohibited. A balloon payment is defined as a lump-sum payment totaling more than twice the amount of your regular payments. Note that HOEPA prohibits balloon payments only when a loan comes due in less than five years; if the loan period is longer than five years, the borrower is not protected by HOEPA.

You may have the right to sue a lender who violates these requirements. If your suit is successful, you may be able to recover statutory and actual damages, court costs, and attorney's fees. (**Statutory damages** are set by law and are, essentially, fines.)

FINANCING SCAMS

If you simply can't get financing through conventional means with reputable lenders, your best bet is to call off the project until you're in a better financial position. If you're in danger of getting in over your head, put your dreams on hold for a while. If you keep pushing for financing, you'll probably find someone who will lend you money—but it could cost you your home.

As a general rule, if you feel pressure from a lender to sign loan documents or you find yourself getting confused, walk out the door—or kick the lender out of your house. A reputable lender will be patient and straight with you.

In addition, be alert to out-and-out scams. There are lots of them, some of which are outlined below:

KEEP THESE WARNING SIGNS IN MIND

Look out for the lender who:

- suggests that you falsify information on a loan application;
- pressures you into applying for more money than you need;
- pressures you into accepting monthly payments you could have trouble making;
- tells you not to bother reading the required loan disclosures;
- misrepresents the kind of credit you're getting, such as referring to a one-time loan as a "line of credit";
- won't give you advance copies of the documents you need to sign;
- promises one set of terms when you apply for a loan, then presents another set of terms at signing; or
- won't give you copies of the documents that you've signed.

Home Equity Stripping

In a home equity stripping scam, a lender talks you into cashing out your equity with a home refinance loan, promising low interest rates and low monthly payments. Then the lender tacks on thousands of dollars in hidden fees and charges, and pushes dozens of documents in front of you to sign without giving you time to read and understand them. Months later, when you discover the true cost of your loans, you may be forced to refinance again. Warning: If you take out a loan but don't have enough income to make the monthly payments, you may have been set up by a dishonest lender, and you may lose your home.

Interest-Only Balloon Loans

With these loans, the payments you make are applied only to the interest on your loan. As a result, when the loan comes due, you still owe the entire amount of the loan principal. Such loans are often secured by your home and are made based on the worth of the home rather than on your creditworthiness or income. As discussed above, any loan that includes balloon payments and is due in less than five years could be covered by HOEPA; if so, you may be able to cancel it. But HOEPA can't protect you if the life of your loan is longer than five years.

Loan Flipping

In a loan flipping scam, a lender calls to talk about refinancing, and tells you it's time the equity in your home started "working" for you. You agree to refinance the loan. After you've made a few payments, the lender calls to offer you a bigger loan. If you accept the offer, he refinances the original loan and then lends you additional money. Each time you refinance, the lender charges you high points and fees, and also may increase your interest rate. If the original loan has a prepayment penalty, you will also have to pay penalty fees each time you take out a new loan.

The Contractor's Home Improvement Loan

Suppose you decide to finance your renovation project through a contractor, and you agree with the contractor on a price for the project. But then, after beginning work, the contractor presents you with loan documents from your lender that indicate higher rates and fees than those that were agreed upon. In this situation, you'll face a difficult choice: sign the papers and accept higher costs, or face the prospect of leaving the renovation unfinished. To avoid this type of situation, you should never finance your home improvement project through a contractor.

Credit Insurance Packing

Credit insurance is a type of insurance that will pay off your debt if you die or become disabled. But purchasing such insurance generally is not a good idea. The sole beneficiary if you die is the lender. And if you become disabled, most credit disability policies protect you only for a limited time, so your loan may not be fully paid off before the insurance runs out. For these reasons, you're much better off going through a regular life insurance company for life and disability insurance.

A lender may tell you that credit insurance comes with your loan, implying that it comes at no additional cost. But of course there is a cost—a lender won't give you insurance of any kind without charging a premium. Should you unwittingly accept the insurance and then object to the added cost, the lender may tell you that the loan papers will have to be rewritten, that the process could take several days, and that the manager may have to reconsider the loan. Don't fall for these scams: just tell your lender that you don't want credit insurance. Period.

HOMEOWNER'S INSURANCE

Before beginning your renovation project, you need to talk with your insurance agent to find out how the project will affect your homeowner's insurance. Most home insurance policies require that you insure your home for a minimum of 80 percent of its replacement value. Thus, any renovation that increases square footage, changes the structure, or otherwise adds value to your home may trigger the need for more insurance coverage. Talk to your agent to discuss all of the possible issues.

Even before work begins on your home, your homeowner's insurance should cover the cost of any building materials on the premises to be used by your contractor. If a fire destroyed both your home and the building materials, you would want to be covered for the full amount of the damages, even if the actual renovation had not yet begun.

Also note that if a renovated or added room is damaged before additional coverage takes effect, you could be responsible for any repair costs.

If your project involves tearing down walls or chimneys,

check your policy for theft and weather damage liability. If you are going to leave your home during the renovation, ask your agent whether your policy includes a vacancy clause; you may not be covered under your homeowner's policy if you are gone for more than thirty days.

Finally, if friends or family members will be helping out with

 TALKING TO A LAWYER

Q. We hired a contractor to renovate our kitchen. He made detailed drawings and sent the plans to the city to obtain a permit. The city denied the permit, citing noncompliance with a number of sections of the building code. We have already paid a 10 percent deposit and advanced fees to the city. Bringing the plan into compliance will involve major changes, and the contractor says he can't do the work for the original contract price. What are our rights?

A. Your only recoverable damages are the 10 percent you paid to the contractor. This is a design/build type of contract, and the contractor's design is inadequate. This means the contractor has breached the contract.

—Answer by John P. Madden, Madden Mediation and Arbitration, Ltd., New York, New York

A. This sounds a bit like a bait and switch. The contractor is supposed to know the building codes. Either he didn't and he is not someone you want building your project; or he did and he is really someone you don't want handling your project. In the latter case he is giving you a low bid to beat legitimate competitors, thinking you will agree to his higher bid when the city turns down the original plan. In either case, you should demand your money (deposit) back and find a reputable contractor. If he refuses, contact the state licensing board.

—Answer by Gerald Niesar, Niesar Curls Bartling, LLP, San Francisco, California the project, you may want to add a personal liability umbrella policy to cover any potential medical bills.

THE WORLD AT YOUR FINGERTIPS

• All the major banks have websites, but the financing information on these sites tends to be very general. For the best information on the types of loans available, and which type will work best for you, talk to a local banker or mortgage broker. Bear in mind that these professionals will likely focus on certain financing methods—usually the ones offered by their employers. So shop around to find the best deal for you.

• For detailed information on federal loan assistance for renovations, go to the U.S. Department of Housing and Urban Development's website at *www.hud.gov*.

• For an excellent discussion of the federal Truth in Lending Act, read "The Federal Truth in Lending Act: What You Don't Know Can Hurt You," by Pamela D. Simmons, available online at *www.abanet.org/rppt/publications/edirt/2005/1/home.html*.

• You can find out more about building permit requirements by visiting the website of your city and county. To find your city's website, type the city name into a search engine, such as *www.google.com*. For example, typing in "City of Sacramento" will return that city's website as the first result. To find your county's website, type the county name and state into a search engine. For example, visiting *www.google.com* and searching for "Cook County Illinois" will return the county website as the first result.

REMEMBER THIS

• Take your time deciding which method of financing is best for you. Be sure that you understand all of the terms of any loan before accepting it. If you have any questions or concerns, talk to an attorney before you sign.

• If you feel any pressure at all from a potential lender to sign loan documents before you have read and understood them, leave the lender's office without signing and don't return.

• The federal Truth in Lending Act protects you. Any lender has to prominently state the annual percentage rate of interest you'll be charged. This means that however you finance your home improvement, you'll know the interest rate. It's up to you to shop for the best terms you can find.

CHAPTER 2

Permits, Licenses, and Other Forms of Permission

Get it Right, or Pay the Price

Ted wanted a shade cover for a small patio in his backyard. A tree would take too long to grow, and there really wasn't a good place for a tree anyway, so Ted decided simply to extend the roof from his family room to cover the patio. A simple enough job, Ted thought; it wouldn't affect the neighbors at all. So he built the roof addition without getting a building permit. But unfortunately for Ted, someone from the town government noticed the roof, checked the building department records, and discovered that the roof had been built without a permit. Now, Ted has bigger problems than a patio without shade. The town insists that he take down the roof and pay a fine. So he's out the money he paid to have the roof built, he has to pay to have the roof extension removed, and he owes the town money for the fine. All that, and he still has no shade for his patio.

While your home may be your castle, it probably doesn't sit on a hill surrounded by a moat. If you have a house, it's probably near other houses; if not, perhaps your home is in the same building as other dwellings. It may be part of a planned development. Your century-old house might lie in a historic district. Or it may be in a municipality that's governed by zoning laws.

The point is that there will almost always be restrictions on what you can do with your home, especially the outside of a house. So let's look at the various forms of consent you'll need in order to renovate your home.

BUILDING PERMITS

A **building permit** is an official document from a municipal building department that authorizes construction work. It is a statement that the building department has seen and approved the plans for the work.

Nearly every city has a department that issues building permits. It may be called the "building department," the "planning department," or something else. Even if you live in an unincorporated town without its own department, the chances are good that such a department exists within your county.

Before embarking on any renovation, you should assume that you need a building permit. If you are making any changes to the structure of your home, you will need a permit. If you are doing work on more than one building (for example, your home and garage), you may need a separate permit for each one, as well as separate permits for specific tasks, such as mechanical, electrical, and plumbing jobs. Even for a project as minor as installing a new window, you may need a permit. For this reason, if you are doing any work to your home at all, you should check with your local building department first. Many city building departments have their own websites, and many of your questions will likely be answered there. But if you're still not sure, pay a visit to the department in person and find out. Remember: Ignorance of the law is no excuse.

Like Ted, many homeowners don't get building permits for home renovation projects because they're unaware that such permits are required. Other homeowners don't get permits because they're afraid their renovations won't be approved. Others just don't want the hassle of dealing with municipal bureaucracy, or of paying permit fees. But if you think getting a permit is a hassle, wait until you see the hassle that results if you get caught without one!

Why does a city care about something as minor as a roof extension, a new toilet, or even a new light switch? Good question.

Cities generally require building permits for two reasons. The first is to ensure that all the buildings constructed in the city are safe and durable—**"up to code"** is the phrase used in the industry. Ensuring that wiring is up to code prevents electrical fires; proper foundations mean stable buildings; good plumbing means safe drinking water and houses that don't flood. The second reason, of course, is that cities need money. A renovated home is often a more valuable home, and a more valuable home means a higher assessment for property taxes. The building permit process allows cities to keep track of the value of the homes in the community, and to assess valuable taxes that ultimately earn the city money.

As a practical matter, your contractor will obtain a building permit for your renovation because:

1. it's part of what a licensed contractor usually does;

2. it's in the contract; and

3. he or she has worked with the building department many times before and knows how to get through the process.

 WHAT DOES "UP TO CODE" MEAN?

Literally, the term "up to code" refers to a building or project that meets the requirements of the city's building code. More than likely, your city uses one of several Uniform Building Codes as the basis for its requirements, and then adds its own specific requirements to form its own unique code. The Uniform Building Codes provide the specifications for building materials and construction technique, from the type of plug fuses to be used for repairing electrical wiring to the maximum water consumption flow rates for replacement toilets (1.6 gallons per flush cycle) and the vertical load requirements for roof supports. Cities then add requirements that fit the particular needs of their local areas. A city in the Midwest, for instance, might add a requirement that water service piping be installed below the level of recorded frost penetration, while a city in California may add requirements to protect buildings against earthquake damage.

A contractor must be licensed in order to take out a permit and work on your house. (Note, however, that you should not take approval of your plans as proof that the contractor is licensed). So if a contractor asks you to obtain a permit on your own, stop everything and check with both your state's contractors licensing board and your city to determine whether the contractor is appropriately licensed. If a contractor tells you that a permit is not required for your project, don't take his or her word for it; check with the building department yourself. Whoever takes out the building permit is held responsible—and accepts the liability—if the work performed does not satisfy local building codes.

The permit must be posted at the job site so that it can be seen from the street. At that point, work can begin. As part of the permit process, the city may inspect the work at different times to ensure that the construction is up to code.

Applying for a Permit

To obtain a permit, a contractor needs to visit the building department, submit a building plan (usually in multiple copies), and provide a good estimate of the construction costs. He or she will also need to provide your assessor's tax parcel number and a full legal description of your property. For smaller projects, a description of the work to be done, plus the application, may be enough. If your plan complies with local codes, the building department will issue a permit for a fee. Look online for the forms and fee schedule for your local jurisdiction. The permit fee offsets the cost of reviewing the plans and the job site inspections.

Inspections

Inspections constitute a major part of the permit process. Generally, your contractor will call the local building department and ask for inspections at different stages of a project. For example, if you're renovating a room, there will be a framing inspection to check the carpentry work and the "rough" electrical

WHAT YOU'LL PAY

In most cities, permit fees are based on estimated construction costs. Cities generally charge a minimum fee, plus a set percentage fee for every $1,000 in construction costs above a certain amount—for example, $12 for every $1,000 in estimated costs above $20,000. There may also be fees for reviewing your plan, additional permit fees for the sub-contracted work (plumbing, electrical, or mechanical), and separate inspection fees. The length of time the building department takes to approve your application depends primarily on the complexity of the project, but for most renovation projects it shouldn't take longer than a few weeks. Your contractor should be able to give you an idea of the wait time after he or she submits your plans to the local department.

work and plumbing before the walls are closed off. If you're adding a room, there will be several additional inspections, including inspections of:

- the footing depths and widths (**footing** is the eight- to ten-inch concrete support for a foundation wall or other structural support);
- the foundation forms;
- the vapor barriers (**vapor barriers** are plastic or foil sheets that are placed between insulation material and the inside of a house; they protect the house against moisture); and
- any below-floor-level electrical, gas, water, or waste piping, and HVAC ducts.

When your project is finished, there will be a final inspection to see that it has been properly completed.

An inspector checks to make sure that work meets local building codes. The inspector will not be concerned with whether you're happy with the work, whether the contractor is meeting your expectations, or even whether the work is of good quality. An inspector's only concern is that the construction is up to code.

WHO ARE THE INSPECTORS?

Inspectors are employees of the local building department, or whichever government department is in charge of code compliance in your area. Depending on the building department, scheduling inspections can be a hassle. Waiting for inspectors can also be a pain in the neck, because work generally can't go forward until an inspector gives the okay.

At each stage of the project, construction cannot proceed without written approval from an inspector indicating that the work has passed inspection. If the work fails to pass inspection at any stage, then work must stop until the necessary changes are made. Obviously, this can throw the project off schedule. Careful adherence to an inspection schedule is one way to monitor the progress of a project.

If you have the money and the inclination, you can also hire an independent inspector to evaluate the quality of your contractor's work as the job progresses. An independent inspector will visit your home at key times during the renovation, and can let you know if there are problems that the contractor needs to address. The inspector's reports can also help later if a formal complaint or lawsuit is filed as a result of shoddy workmanship. Inspectors charge roughly $800 to $1,500 to oversee a project, depending on its complexity.

If You Don't Have a Permit...

If you don't have a permit for your project, you may face some serious consequences. In the worst of all possible worlds, you could be forced to tear down the construction, apply for a permit, redo the job, and pay penalties and fines. If electrical wiring has been performed without a permit, your city could force you to open the wall so that the wiring can be inspected, and make you pay for the inspection. If an inspector decides the work performed on your project is illegal, he or she can stop the current renovation work and force you to bring the work up to code before the project can go forward. This may mean tearing down walls or even tearing out the old work and replacing it. If you are responsible for illegal work, you could be held liable for punitive permit fees and additional fines.

Even if your illegal renovation does not appear on your city's radar screen immediately, it may turn into a blip when you go to sell your home. When selling a home, the seller is required to disclose any conditions that might affect the home's value. If the buyer or the buyer's inspector notices changes that were made without a permit, the sale could be killed—especially if the seller knew about the work. The appraiser for the buyer's bank may also want to see permit records to check the legality of any renovations. If no permits are found and it's obvious that the home has been renovated, the bank will likely refuse to make the loan. If the illegal work is not discovered until after closing, the home's value could become a matter of litigation.

ZONING

Don't confuse building permits with zoning requirements. The building department focuses on the quality of the construction relating to your project. The zoning department, on the other hand, is concerned about the different areas of your city as parts of a whole. So even though the building department may grant you a permit to build an additional bedroom, the zoning department may not allow it.

How Zoning Works

The main purpose of zoning is to organize cities, so that residential neighborhoods are separate from the industrial parts of cities, and downtown business districts aren't broken up by single-family homes. Practically speaking, this means that if your neighborhood is zoned residentially, you won't have to

A QUICK LOOK AT ZONING LAWS

A zoning ordinance consists of a map and text. The zoning map shows the division of the city into different districts and their usage. Most zoning ordinances include residential, commercial, industrial, and agricultural districts. The zoning map must show precise boundaries for each district.

The zoning text that accompanies the map explains the zoning rules for each district. These rules list the permitted uses of the land in each district and specific standards governing lot size, building height, and yard and setback provisions.

Residential districts, in turn, are often broken down further into zones for single-family and multi-family dwellings.

---

worry about someone building a gas station next door. Another purpose of zoning is to control the character of neighborhoods. This means that you may not be able to do everything you might want to do with your home.

Zoning regulations are concerned with the impact your house, or additions to your house, may have on your neighbors and the neighborhood. Most zoning ordinances regulate, for instance, the distance between a house and its property line. So if your planned bedroom addition will cause your house to extend too close to your neighbor's line, the size or dimensions of the addition will have to be changed. A city's zoning laws also might specify, for example, the type of material you can use for a new fence, how close the fence can be to the street, whether you can put a fence in your front yard, and how high the fence can be.

Most residential districts mandate a minimum lot width and depth, the amount of a lot that can be taken up by a house, and the minimum distance that a house may be set back from the street. Such districts may even regulate the size of a house's dormers (a **dormer** is a window with its own roof).

Zoning laws also regulate the way in which you use your home. A new home office may be acceptable if you're a freelance writer, for example, but zoning regulations may not allow the office if you'll have a steady stream of clients, because that could have an impact on traffic and parking in your neighborhood.

Is There a Way to Deal With Zoning Restrictions?

You can get around zoning restrictions by applying to your local zoning board for a variance. A **variance** is approval from a zoning board to deviate from its regulations. As part of the process, you may need to give notice to your neighbors of the proposed change, so that they have an opportunity to object, and you may need to attend a public hearing before the zoning board. Generally, variances are granted in cases where a hardship exists due to the shape, condition, or location of a property. For purposes of obtaining a variance, a **hardship** is a difficulty with your property that you have not created yourself. You will also have to convince the board that your proposed renovation will not change the character of your neighborhood or reduce its property values.

 EASEMENTS

Easements grant someone else a right to use part of your property for a specific purpose. They're recorded at the county courthouse and normally turn up in a title search. Easements can be either public or private. Public easements allow, for example, a power company to run a power line over your backyard, or the city to run a sewer line under your backyard. Private easements typically relate to access. For instance, a private easement might allow your neighbor to use a path through your property to reach an alley. While easements themselves aren't likely to create any problems for your renovation, keep in mind that your permit may be denied if the renovation will change the size or dimensions of your home and cause it to encroach on an easement.

TALKING TO A LAWYER

Q. When we applied for a permit to build a bathroom in our basement, the building department would not issue it because it found that there was no record of a finished basement. The building department wants to inspect the entire basement to see if it is up to code before we can build the bathroom. None of this was disclosed when we bought the house ten years ago. Are we required to pay everything it takes to bring our house up to code?

A. Probably, and recourse against the seller is unlikely because of the length of time that has elapsed since you purchased the home.

Q. One side of our house, which is seventy-five years old, sits about eight feet from the property line. Our zoning laws now require that buildings be at least ten feet from the property line. We are planning to build an addition that would extend the side of the house farther down our property. The contractor says we don't need a variance, because the house is already less than ten feet from the line, and we would just be continuing an existing deviation from the zoning laws. Do we need to apply for a variance?

A. Yes. The original house is most likely "grandfathered"—which means that imposing the zoning restriction against the existing structure would be void as an ex post facto law. However, the new addition would be subject to review and would require a variance.

—Answers by R. Stephen Hansell, lawyer, patent attorney, and construction arbitrator, Florence, Montana

NEIGHBORS

When considering renovation, don't forget about your neighbors. After all, renovation doesn't just mean that your home is going to be messy for a while; it also means that the neighbors may have to put up with inconveniences such as dust and noise, a Dumpster in your driveway, and trucks driving in and out of the neighborhood to drop lumber in your yard. Talk to them ahead of time and let them know what you're planning. It's a matter of courtesy, but not a bad strategic move, either. If you're planning an addition that needs a zoning variance, your neighbors could create trouble for you and your project if they object to the variance. As is the case with so many factors in the renovation process, simple and courteous communication can prevent most problems.

HISTORIC DISTRICTS

Historic districts are generally established by states to preserve the character of old neighborhoods and buildings. If your home is a historic building or is located in a historic district,

A HISTORIC HOUSE MIGHT GET YOU A GRANT

Surprisingly, if you own a home that is listed on the National Register of Historic Places, there are no restrictions on your ability to renovate or even demolish the home (though there might well be such restrictions if your building is in a local historic zone). However, it might be worth your while to renovate appropriately. If your home is listed on the National Register, and you renovate the home according to federal guidelines, then you may be eligible for a federal preservation grant covering 50 percent of the cost of your project.

You can nominate your own property to be on the National Register by mailing a nomination to the State Historic Preservation Officer (SHPO) in your state (visit *www.cr.nps.gov/nr/listing.htm* for more information). The SHPO may then nominate the property for inclusion on the National Register. In order to nominate your home, you must be able to document the historical significance of the property in accordance with certain criteria established by the National Register.

you could be restricted from altering its exterior appearance. Historic districts are governed by district commissions, which are very similar to zoning boards. Their purpose is to make certain that any exterior changes to buildings in the district stay within that district's character. This can—and, in some places, does—mean that even minor details like doorknobs and paint colors will be regulated. The jurisdiction of district commissions is similar to that of zoning boards, but is more focused on aesthetic issues.

If your house is in a local historic district, the historic commission may want the house to retain a semblance of its original appearance, and may thus require your renovation to "blend in" with the original structure. However, district commissions generally do not review repair and maintenance projects in which no material or design changes are made.

 TALKING TO A LAWYER

Q. *We live in a historic district in a one-hundred-year-old house. The original tile roof on our house is starting to fall apart, and we experience serious leaking every time it rains. We applied for a permit to replace the roof with an architectural shingle, which will be a lot less expensive than a tile roof, and the city referred us to the historic district commission. The commission has told us that we are required to have a tile roof to retain the character of the district. Do we have legal recourse?*

A. Yes. The commission's decision can be appealed to a court of competent jurisdiction. Note, however, that the commission's discretion usually will be upheld, unless it is unreasonable or unsupported.

—**Answer by R. Stephen Hansell, lawyer, patent attorney, and construction arbitrator, Florence, Montana**

COMMUNITY LIVING

Community living is becoming an increasingly common way of life. Condominiums, cooperative apartments in urban areas, and planned unit developments in the suburbs are all forms of shared ownership, which sometimes brings with it severe restrictions on your ability to do what you want with your home. If you are involved in any kind of community living arrangement, you will likely need the approval of a governing board—a condominium association board, a cooperative corporation board, or, in a planned unit development, a homeowners' association—in order to undertake renovations.

An appealing feature of common-interest communities, especially planned unit developments, is their consistent "look." During the planning stages of your project, you need to think about whether your renovation will fit in with that look. There is generally a lot of give-and-take among owners in such communities, because denying your neighbor's request to renovate could mean that your neighbor will deny you a similar request in the future. Thus, if your renovation is in keeping with the feel of your community and doesn't interfere with your neighbors' enjoyment, you should be in good shape to win acceptance of your plan.

As a matter of common sense, talk to your neighbors and governing board members as you're starting to plan your renovation. Make sure your project follows the necessary rules. Give your neighbors a chance to voice any objections before you begin work, and modify your plans if you think their concerns are reasonable. You're much better off reaching an informal compromise before you go to the board, rather than taking your chances with a board ruling. If you think your neighbors are being unreasonable, prepare to counter their arguments when you bring your project before the board.

If the board rejects your renovation proposal, you may have a difficult time getting that decision overturned. The reason is that, in condos, co-ops, and planned unit developments, unit owners agree to abide by the rules and decisions of elected board members. Because of this agreement, courts generally adopt a hands-off approach when it comes to reviewing board decisions—an approach that recognizes the need for rules and management discretion, and defers to the technical expertise of the administrative body.

In cases that do come before the courts, courts generally are guided in their decision making by two legal principles: the rule of reasonableness and, in some states, the business judgment rule. In practice, board decisions rarely get overturned.

Discussions of the **rule of reasonableness** generally involve a lot of "lawyer-speak," but the basic question a court will seek to answer is: Was the board's decision reasonable? The answer hinges on whether a court thinks a "reasonably prudent" board would have made that same decision.

The "reasonable person" standard has been a fixture of the law for centuries, and cases of this sort are no exception. At its core, the question of whether a decision is reasonable is a question of whether it was made using common sense and good faith. Over the years, as more and more cases involving the decision-making power of condominium boards have come before the courts, those courts have begun to develop a consensus as to what constitutes reasonable behavior in this context. This standard can then be applied to new situations as they arise. For example: Is there a legitimate purpose to the rule that all electrical work in a condo must be done by a licensed electrician? Does it make sense that a unit owner should be responsible for the removal and disposal of hazardous materials exposed during a renovation? Is it reasonable to demand that a unit owner post a bond worth twice the value of a proposed renovation?

Generally, courts applying the **business judgment rule** will assume that the directors of a corporation—or, in this case, the members of a board: (1) act in good faith; and (2) act in the best business interests of their corporation—or, in this case, community—when they make a discretionary decision. (In this context, a **discretionary decision** is any decision that a board has authority to make under the terms of its master deed and bylaws.) Therefore, in order to convince a court to reverse a board's decision under the business judgment rule, a unit owner would have to show that the board lacked good faith (for example, acted with malice), discriminated against the owner, or acted illegally. You might also prevail if you can show that the board failed to follow its own rules, regulations, or established precedents. If the board has the authority to make a decision for or against you—or to exercise its discretion by, say, limiting the size of your renovation—then an argument that the board made a mistake simply because it disagreed with you is not going to carry the day in court.

Condominiums

According to the Uniform Common Interest Ownership Act, a **condominium** is "a common interest community in which portions of the real estate are designated for separate ownership and the remainder of the real estate is designated for common ownership solely by the owners of those portions."

This means that individual condominium owners own their individual units and share ownership of "common elements"— the hallways, walkways, utilities, and building structures. What's important here is that an individual unit consists only of the space within its exterior walls—that is, the exterior walls comprise its boundaries. Typical boundary surfaces include the upper plane of the floor underlayment, and the painted surface of a ceiling or outside wall. The default boundary of the unit— that is, the boundary unless the condominium documents indicate otherwise, which they often do—is the imaginary plane formed by the faces of the studs in a unit's wall. This means that if you drive a nail into the wall of your condo to hang a picture, and the nail goes into the stud, you may have breached your property line.

In a condominium, each unit owner holds the title to his or her unit, but title to the land, building, exteriors, recreational areas, and other facilities intended for common use is held by all the unit owners in common. Ownership of the common elements is divided proportionately, based on the value of the units.

A master deed divides the property into units and common elements and states the rights, obligations, and restrictions of unit owners. Bylaws and a certificate of incorporation govern the formation and operation of the condominium association, its administrative functions, and the rights and duties of directors, officers and members.

Cooperatives

The Uniform Common Interest Ownership Act defines a **cooperative** as "a common interest community in which the real estate is owned by an association, each of whose members is entitled by virtue of his ownership interest in the association to exclusive possession of a unit."

This means that individual unit owners technically don't own their units; rather, they own shares in the co-op, which entitles them to occupy their units under so-called **proprietary leases**. Essentially, the co-op functions as a corporation in which the owner of each unit has a percentage interest. The size of a person's interest is based on the size of his or her unit, which means that owners of smaller units have fewer shares in the corporation, but pay a smaller portion of the assessments than do the larger units. (This is also true of condominiums.)

As is the case with condos, the common elements in a co-op include all property not owned or occupied by a unit owner. The boundaries in a co-op are not drawn as precisely as they are in condos; thus, issues like the precise plane formed by a unit's studs are of less concern in the co-op context than in the context of condos. Instead, because of the peculiar ownership structure, boundary issues are governed by rules resembling those of landlord-tenant law, with the unit owners treated as tenants and the corporation treated as a landlord. As a practical matter, this means that—depending on what's in the proprietary lease—the co-op corporation may be able to regulate even such minor issues as the color of paint and wallpaper inside your unit.

The Governing Documents

Before you start renovating your condo or co-op, read your condo association's **covenants, conditions, and restrictions (CCRs)** or your co-op's proprietary lease to see if your association will allow your proposed project. Associations usually have very specific regulations concerning changes to a unit's interior or exterior. The rules will vary, but are likely to impose restrictions on renovation and noise levels. If you want to make any changes to the structure of your unit, such as taking out pipes and ducts or knocking down walls, you will probably need the permission of the association board. Remember, in a condo, you only own what's on your side of the walls. Don't assume that what you want to do is okay; instead, assume that you will need the board's permission. As a condo or co-op owner, you're going to have to jump through some extra hoops to get your renovation project going.

Most condo and co-op associations issue a standard alteration agreement to cover renovation issues before they arise. A typical alteration agreement requires unit owners to pay for any legal, engineering, or architectural advice that the board needs in making its determinations for approval. Many agreements also require the unit owner to indemnify the association for any damage caused during work. Alteration agreements also can limit the hours during which demolition and construction work can take place, set forth appropriate methods for removing demolition debris, specify which parts of the common area can be used by workers and delivery people, and address any number of other issues relating to the safety and the livability of the building. A board may also require the unit owner to put up a bond to cover any damage caused by the construction. The alteration agreement is a contract, which means that if a unit owner violates the agreement, the violation may be considered a breach of the master deed or proprietary lease.

As a unit owner, you should make sure that your construction contract covers the terms of your alteration agreement. For example, if your agreement prohibits Dumpsters from being placed in common areas, or if the board doesn't want a Dumpster sitting in front of your building for the duration of the demolition, your contractor will have to move the waste every day, which is an added expense. Be sure to work that cost into the construction contract. In addition, the board should review the construction contract before the work begins, and may also have an engineer or architect review the plans.

If your condo building is an apartment building, you'll need to arrange entry for the workers each day during your project, and make sure they are covered by insurance for the time they're going to spend in the building.

Another serious concern of the association will be proper payment of the contractor by the unit owner. The reason for this concern is that, if the unit owner and contractor disagree and the unit owner withholds payment, the contractor could slap a

 TALKING TO A LAWYER

Q. I live in a five-unit condo. Two of the roofs had leaks, so the homeowners' association hired a roofer to fix the roof. The roofer said that in order to fix the roof over the two units, he needed to redo the entire roof because we all share a wall. After he finished, I had a leak in my roof. What are my rights?

A. Roofs are a homeowners' association issue. The roof should be fixed, repaired, and brought into satisfactory condition by the homeowners' association. If any damage was done to your condo's interior as a result of the leaky roof, you will have to submit a claim under your own homeowner's insurance. Your insurance company may subsequently be able to recover from the roofer, if the interior damage occurred due to the roofer's poor work.

—**Answer by Gerald Niesar, Niesar Curls Bartling, LLP,**
San Francisco, California

mechanic's lien on the building, which could create financing problems for the association. In light of this, requirements for prompt payment should be carefully spelled out in your construction contract. The board may also require the unit holder to post a bond to cover the lien—or, where local law allows, may require the contractor and subcontractors to waive their rights to a mechanic's lien.

Planned Unit Development

The planned unit development (PUD) concept has been applied primarily to new subdivisions of vacant land. Housing in a PUD is clustered so that individual lots are smaller than standard lots, but open space is preserved as a common area. In a PUD, an individual owns a unit—similar to the condominium concept, except that the unit is a plot of land—and either the corporation or the unit owners collectively have title to the common areas.

Restrictive Covenants

While zoning restrictions are imposed by governments, PUDs come with private restrictions called **restrictive covenants**. Restrictive covenants are usually drawn up by developers to maintain quality control over neighborhoods, and may restrict your ability to use your land in certain ways, even if zoning laws would otherwise permit the use. A **covenant** ("covenant" is really just another word for "contract") is an agreement between a homeowner and the homeowners' association—or, if there is no such association, the neighbors. You should ask for a copy of the covenant before you buy your home, because it's part of the purchase package—and you need to see it to know that you will be comfortable with the restrictions. You will also receive a copy of the covenant when you purchase your home.

Though the point of a restrictive covenant is to prevent your next-door neighbor from growing unkempt prairie grass on his lawn or turning his front yard into an auto body shop, covenants may also specify such details as the size of lots in the PUD, the minimum square footage of its houses, the design of the houses, the types of fences you can build, and sometimes even the color you can paint your house.

As is the case with condo and co-op associations, you will need to receive approval from the homeowners' association before you can proceed with your renovation. Restrictive covenants may be enforced by a court if negotiations fail and a neighbor who objects to a violation of the covenant files a lawsuit.

RENOVATING RENTAL PROPERTY

The fundamental fact about being a tenant is that you don't own the property in which you live. As a result, there really is nothing you can do to renovate your rental home unless the landlord approves. So before you start renovating a rental, do yourself a favor and read your lease. The chances are very good that the lease will forbid you to remodel or make any structural changes without the landlord's prior written permission.

From the landlord's perspective, having a tenant renovate his or her rental home is not an attractive idea. As owners of their property, landlords are responsible for following building codes and zoning ordinances, and for making sure that certain repairs and renovations are done correctly. If you mess up the landlord's property (through, say, a small plumbing job gone awry), the landlord is stuck with the problem—after you've been evicted, of course! If a tenant fails to pay a contractor, then the landlord could be subject to a mechanic's lien.

What about the other way around? What if the landlord wants to renovate your rental home while you're living there? If the renovation is necessary—for instance, if the landlord needs to bring the electrical wiring up to code—then the landlord is allowed to do the work. If you're unable to occupy your home while the work is being completed, then in many cities you'll be entitled to a relocation payment, or the landlord will have to find you suitable, equivalent housing while the repairs are being made. If the work is not necessary to bring your home up to code, then you, as the tenant, can refuse permission.

Let's return to the scenario in which you, the tenant, have proposed a renovation. If the landlord agrees to your renovation plan, you will need to write up a request for consent and have your landlord sign it. In the request, specify in detail what work will be done. And be sure to keep notes of all your conversations about the renovation with the landlord.

Remember that you, as the tenant, do not own the property. So go ahead and renovate, but remember: If the finished product is part of your home, it stays when you leave. Anything permanent in the home—that is, anything attached in any manner to the walls, ceiling, or floor—is considered a **fixture**, and belongs to the owner of the home. If you install track lighting or put in a new countertop in the kitchen, your improvement will ultimately belong to the landlord. Depending on your ability to negotiate, the landlord may agree to reimburse you for your costs or reduce your rent, but remember that the landlord receives the ultimate benefit of any improvements you make. On the other hand, improvements that are not attached to the house, such as bookcases and appliances, remain yours when you leave.

Finally, note that commercial leases often provide that property be restored to its original condition before the lease term ends.

THE WORLD AT YOUR FINGERTIPS

• Your first stop online should be the Permit Place website at *www.permitplace.com/links/search1.asp*. It provides links to state, county, and city websites that contain information on permits and licensing.

• There are many helpful municipal websites that will answer questions and provide examples of the requirements and application forms for building permits. For a great example, visit *www.ci.austin.tx.us/development/bpinfo1.htm*. The City of Evanston,

Illinois also has good resources online; visit *www.cityofevanston* *.org*, click on "Resident," and choose "Building" from the drop-down menu.

• The MegaLaw website, at *www.megalaw.com*, features comprehensive lists of condominium and zoning laws from around the country, as well as dozens of articles related to condominium and zoning law.

• To read the Uniform Common Interest Ownership Act for yourself, visit this website sponsored by the University of Pennsylvania:

www.law.upenn.edu/bll/ulc/fnact99/1990s/ucioa94.htm.

REMEMBER THIS

• If you renovate without a building permit, you could face fines and penalties, and could even be forced to tear down and rebuild your renovation. The permit process can be slow and irritating, but it's not worth the trouble to avoid it.

• If your renovation affects the exterior of your home, be sure to run your plans by the zoning department.

• Your renovation is very likely to be an inconvenience to your neighbors. Before you start renovating, it's a good idea to pay them a courtesy call. Let them know what you'll be doing and how long the project will last, and give them a chance to voice their concerns.

• If you live in a community ownership building or development, remember to review the applicable covenants, conditions, and restrictions before proceeding with your planning.

CHAPTER 3

Do It Yourself

From Scheduling to Subcontractors

Steve is a terrific handyman. He can build anything, fix anything, and his basement is filled with all sorts of power saws and power drills. He's an excellent carpenter, a good plumber, and a good electrician. The deck he built for his father was perfect. So when Steve decided to expand his kitchen to accommodate his growing family, he figured he knew enough about building to handle the project himself. And then the fun began.

If, like Steve, you are a skilled amateur carpenter-plumber-electrician, you might want to do your renovation yourself. If you have the skill, experience, and time to spare, then you could save some money by completing the project on your own. However, if your renovation is extensive, you'll need to do some careful planning and preparation. A larger do-it-yourself project will require you to do all the work of a contractor—from drawing up plans to coordinating and managing multiple subcontractors.

This chapter will discuss the many issues you'll face if you're doing your own renovation or acting as your own contractor—including plans, costs, permits, appliances, scheduling, and subcontractor management.

BEFORE YOU START

Before you make the decision to renovate your home yourself, you may want to consider the following questions:

1. Do you know what you're doing? In the case of a large project, it's not enough to be a decent amateur carpenter—you need to know how to plan the renovation, as well as do the work. If you have some experience, and the renovation you've planned isn't too complex, go for it. One note of caution, though: If

you're thinking of selling your home somewhere down the line, your workmanship is going to be on display for potential buyers. If you don't do the job right, it could cost you money later.

2. Do you have the tools and equipment to do the work? When you think about the project, think about the tools you will need. If you don't have the tools, you can always buy them or even rent them—but remember that buying or renting new tools is an expense that will make your do-it-yourself job more costly.

3. Will it take longer? If you complete the project yourself, you probably won't be saving time. In fact, chances are that a do-it-yourself project will take several times longer than the same project performed by a contractor. On the other hand, spreading the project over time can also enable you to spread out the cost.

4. How much will it cost? By doing the work yourself, you'll be trading money for time. You'll be saving on contractor's fees and the subcontractors' labor costs. You won't be receiving the contractor discount on materials, but that could be a wash, since you also won't be paying the contractor's markup on materials. As with any other project, you should make a budget and stick to it, and count on the project costing at least 20 percent more than you anticipate. Keep in mind that if you make a mistake and have to redo something, you'll have to pay for it.

5. Will you need a building permit? Even minor home renovations, such as replacing a toilet or repairing a broken window, may require a building permit. Depending on the nature of your renovation, you may have to involve an architect to draw up plans in order to get one.

6. Do you have sufficient insurance? Check with your insurance agent to see if your homeowner's policy provides sufficient coverage. If you're having friends come over to help you out, make sure that you have coverage for them as well.

7. Do you need a variance? If the project expands the exterior walls of your home, you may need a variance or a special design review from your local planning commission. If you live in a planned development, the homeowners' association may have review rights for any exterior work.

⚠ ACTING AS YOUR OWN GENERAL CONTRACTOR

It's one thing to take on all the physical work yourself, if you know what you're doing with hammers, saws, and all the tools of the trade. But in terms of difficulty, managing your own contracting project is in a whole other league. Being a general contractor has little to do with handling a hammer and nails well. It's a different skill—as different as being a good baseball player is from being a good manager of a baseball team.

A homeowner who becomes his or her own general contractor has to understand construction. To the layperson, "construction" simply means "building things." But as a business, which is what you're getting into, construction also involves work sequencing. It involves management of resources—including money, equipment, and people. A general contractor often doesn't hammer any nails or install any pipes; rather, the contractor is an engineer of organization and schedule. The contractor has to know how much time each part of the job should take, who is capable of doing the work, who is available to do the work, and in what order the jobs need to be performed.

There's an old saw in the legal profession that a lawyer who represents himself has a fool for a client. While it may not be equally foolish to do your own general contracting, it nonetheless requires a great deal of knowledge that you may not possess, a great deal of work, and a great deal of financial and legal risk.

PLANS

Whether you're doing your renovation yourself or acting as your own contractor and bringing in subcontractors, the first question you will face is whether you should draw up the plans for your renovation, or bring in an architect.

If you're planning to build additions to your existing home, then you'll need to hire an architect; most building departments will not accept plans for filing which do not bear the seal of a licensed architect or engineer. If you're simply remodeling the interior of your home, you may be able to manage without an architect; in the case of remodeling jobs, most building departments will accept detailed drawings or plans that an architect has not approved. However, be warned that the building department will require the plans for a remodeling job to be very specific—the department must be able to determine from the plans whether your project will affect plumbing and wiring, and whether it will create any structural problems. If you can't draw plans that answer these kinds of questions, then you'll need to bring in an architect after all.

Here's what an architect can do for you: The architect's job is to plan your space and understand the options presented by that space. An architect, by instinct and training, can visualize what a finished space will look like. He or she can mentally knock down walls and empty out existing rooms. The architect can understand the possibilities of a room, the problems created by that room, and how to solve those problems ahead of time. This is not to say that architects never engage in overdesign, but they can show homeowners the possibilities for their homes and lay out solid plans for their renovation.

If the architect's plans call for a more expensive project than you've planned for, then the project can be scaled back by cutting back on the quality of the materials, eliminating fea-

 FINDING YOUR COMFORT ZONE

The level of the architect's participation in your project is up to you and the architect—whatever works best for the two of you. The architect can simply provide you with plans and withdraw from the project as soon as the building permit is issued, or he or she can stick with the project as a consultant or project administrator who drops by once a week or at critical junctures in the work process.

tures from your finished design, or simplifying the plan to better match your budget.

COST

You're going to have to figure out how much your renovation will cost. If you're doing the renovation yourself, then the total cost will equal the cost of materials plus the value of your time. In addition, you will have to think about what unforeseen conditions (problems) may be hiding behind the walls—such as mold, faulty wiring, or rotted wood—and what those problems might do to your budget. This should be a primary concern when performing any type of renovation on an older home.

 WAYS TO CUT COSTS

When thinking about renovating your home, consider everything involved—including how to finance your project. Your aim is to balance costs with quality. Keep in mind that what's cheapest in the short term may prove to be more expensive if the materials or workmanship fall apart. To help keep a lid on costs, you should make a budget and research all the costs involved with your renovation to come up with a reasonable estimate. In your estimate, include:

- labor
- tools and equipment
- materials
- permits
- cleanup

It's not uncommon for projects to cost 20 percent to 30 percent more than anticipated, so factor in this extra amount in order to obtain a realistic estimate.

If you're bringing in subcontractors to do some of the work, then you will need to have a good idea of how long it takes a carpenter to frame out and finish a room, how long it will take a plumber to move the plumbing around, and so on (see the section on scheduling later in this chapter). And, of course, you need to know what each subcontractor charges per hour. In most geographical areas, average renovation costs are based on square footage; this type of information can be obtained from a reliable contractor, architect, or real estate agent. An architect can also help with cost estimates, though he or she is typically not as close to the day-to-day work as a contractor, and thus might overlook some costs.

Once you have an idea of what your project will cost, it will be time to go to the bank. You'll probably need to finance the renovation through a bank or other lender, unless you have plenty of cash available.

INSURANCE

If you're bringing in subcontractors to help with your renovation, then you will need to beef up your insurance. Make sure you're covered for injuries the workers might suffer on the job (workers' compensation), and for damage they might cause to third parties (general liability coverage). You can find more information about these forms of insurance in chapter 4. Check with your insurance agent to see if your homeowner's policy covers you as an employer; if not, arrange to get temporary coverage. And you will need to talk to your accountant about whether your legal relationship with the subcontractors raises any tax issues.

PERMITS

Before beginning your project, you will need to get a building permit from the city building or planning department. If you live in a historic preservation district, your local historic commission may need an application as well. If you live in a condo, co-op, or planned development, those boards must also grant consent. If exterior work (other than painting) is involved, the zoning department must also review the project for setbacks, proper uses of the property, and parking requirements. If your house is in a historic preservation district, the historic commission will also need to conduct another review of any work to the exterior. Most cities can provide a checklist of information and required documents, which will differ depending on the scope of your project. Remodeling a single-family kitchen, for example, will call for a different checklist than remodeling a single family bathroom.

To get a permit, you will need to (1) fill out a permit application; and (2) submit detailed plans or sketches showing the proposed work. Depending on the nature of the work, you may need to hire an architect to draw up your plans (see discussion above). If you are using subcontractors, you will also need to submit subcontractor worksheets, which list in detail the scope of the work to be performed and the materials to be used. Chapter 2 contains more information on permits, zoning, and other forms of permission you may need.

BUYING APPLIANCES AND FIXTURES

Before you head down to the appliance store or research major appliances, look at your plans and walk through the space you're going to renovate. You need to look at every part of your space from every possible angle, because everything in the room requires a decision. "Coordination" and "integration" are the watchwords here. Stop every few steps to consider the space from every perspective. There are dozens of decisions to be made: if the refrigerator is there, what does that do to the rest of the kitchen? When you open the refrigerator, will the door bang into something? How big should the sink be? What are the standard sizes of sinks? How much more does a custom sink cost? What kind of faucet do you want? What kind of faucet can you afford? Wood floor? Tile floor? What are the implications of having a wood floor in the kitchen? Would it be easier to keep clean? Would it be more likely to stain?

Once you have made your basic decisions, break out the measuring tape. Be very precise with your measurements. A stove that sticks out even one inch beyond the adjacent counter-top can drive you crazy. A refrigerator that's an inch too wide won't fit in the space you've made for it. Remember to keep the electrical outlets in mind when planning where to position the appliances.

Finally, you'll be ready to buy. It may make sense to buy appliances yourself even if you have a contractor, because you'll avoid the contractor's markup. With wholesale home stores in every corner of the country, you will likely be able to buy the same appliances the contractor would buy for you, only for less money. In addition, because it is now possible to buy appliances online for a discount, it's worth browsing a bit on the Web to see what's available. But as with all Internet purchases, be careful. The greatest danger of purchasing something online is that you often don't know whether a seller is reliable or honest. Is the supplier affiliated with a major appliance manufacturer? Will your goods be shipped on time? Can you return an item if it's defective? The Internet is a great place to spend time before visiting a dealer, but it may not be the best place to buy.

All major appliances come with a **manufacturer's warranty** (also called a **factory warranty**) that covers all costs for parts and labor for a limited period of time—typically one year, and five years for major parts. Make sure your warranty, like most warranties, covers the costs of in-home service. Be sure to read the warranty to make sure you understand it before you buy. Try to anticipate problems that may arise. For example, if you purchase a toilet from a home store, and the toilet is cracked when you pull it out of the box, can you return it to the store and exchange it? Do you have to go through the manufacturer?

In addition, manufacturers and many appliance stores will offer extended warranties that cover parts and labor beyond the term of the manufacturer's warranty. The most important consideration is who is offering the warranty. The manufacturer is most likely to give you the best service, because it knows its own product better than anyone else, and has a vested interest in satisfying its customers. A warranty from a local dealer can be a good choice, but make sure the dealer will be personally performing the service. Many dealers offer warranties that are serviced by independent third parties; be wary of these. If a third-party company disappears, your warranty may not be valid. And, as always, read the warranty contract and understand before you sign what it does and doesn't cover.

SCHEDULING

You'll need to create a rough schedule for your project, keeping in mind the sequence in which the work must be completed. This means that you have to understand the work sequence, and the requirements for each stage of the work. For example, before you build anything, you'll probably have to tear something down. It doesn't take a lot of skill to break things up, but you do want to make sure you don't crack a load-bearing wall in the course of your demolition. Once a wall is demolished, the resulting mess has to be carted off by someone to somewhere. These are the types of issues you will need to address.

Scheduling is particularly important if you are acting as a contractor and overseeing the work of subcontractors. For the do-it-yourself contractor, scheduling can be especially challenging. The drywaller can't come in until the plumber finishes, and the plumber can't start until the carpenter finishes the framing. If the plumber shows up at the house as scheduled, but the framing hasn't been completed, two problems can result. First, the homeowner may be charged for the visit, because the plumber has wasted his time mobilizing for a job he can't yet do—and, depending on the contract, he or she may be well within his rights to charge for the wasted hours. Second, just because the plumber was available on Wednesday

TALKING TO A LAWYER

Q. *I am renovating two bathrooms. I'm going to buy all the fixtures and do the carpentry work myself, but I need to hire a plumber and an electrician. For the plumbing, I was planning to call a large plumbing contractor in town and have one of its employees do the work. The electrician I plan to hire has his own business, a one-man shop. What are my legal obligations in each of these relationships?*

A. The legal obligations in each of these relationships will depend upon the contract that you execute with both contractors. More than likely, each contractor will present you with his or her own standard contract. You should be a bit leery of these documents, as they are usually skewed in favor of the contractor. Make sure that each document includes: provisions for adequate insurance coverage for the contractor; appropriate indemnity provisions to protect you from third-party claims; a specific description of the scope of work to be performed and materials to be used by the contractor; a schedule for the contractor; and a statement of which party will have control over the schedule. Obviously, problems with an agreement of this nature can have serious legal consequences. Spending a little money on an attorney who is experienced in construction contracting may avoid costly problems down the road.

—Answer by Darren Duzyk, Sullivan & Duzyk, Lexington, Kentucky

does not mean he or she will be able to return to your house on Thursday. Like all subcontractors, plumbers get paid by the hour, so they are constantly lining up work. This means that if you miss the plumber on Wednesday, you may not see that plumber again until the following Tuesday. And if you have to reschedule the plumber, then you'll have to reschedule the drywaller, too.

WORKING WITH SUBCONTRACTORS

If you're planning to bring in subcontractors to work on your renovation, many questions and issues will arise. The first question is: Who should you hire? Should you hire a general handyman? In most states, any project costing more than $500 requires the use of licensed contractors. There's another concern with hiring a handyman. Because an unlicensed handyman cannot legally be a contractor under many states' laws, the legal status of a handyman will be that of an employee, a status that can subject the homeowner to unemployment insurance and income tax withholding requirements. So, no—don't hire a handyman to renovate your kitchen.

Should you hire unlicensed subcontractors? Absolutely not—for legal reasons, insurance reasons, and because it's just plain common sense. If a plumber is too lazy to take a state licensing test, you probably don't want that plumber in charge of moving the water in your house. Stick with licensed professionals who are properly insured.

Think about how to deal with subcontractors before you begin. One important practical consideration is that a homeowner's contractual control over subcontractors lasts only for the duration of a single job. That's not a legal issue. But it means that, unlike a general contractor, you will not be providing your subcontractors with continuing work and income. As a result, they may not be as responsive to you. If a subcontractor is squeezed for time and must decide between working for a homeowner and working for a general contractor, the general contractor will win every time. That's just good business for the subcontractor. But it's not good news for the homeowner.

You're going to have to spend a lot of time supervising your subcontractors. A contractor can't just hire a bunch of guys and turn them loose; rather, the job will not be done properly without a great deal of oversight. A major difference between a homeowner and a general contractor is that the contractor will likely have an existing working relationship with the subcontrac-

TALKING TO A LAWYER

Q. I am assembling a group of subcontractors to build a large addition to my home. I will be doing some of the work, but most of it will be done by the subcontractors while I am at my office during the day. How often do I need to be physically present while the work is proceeding? What I really want to do is hire someone to stop by every morning and directly supervise by phone all day. Am I setting myself up for legal problems?

A. You are likely setting yourself up for timing, work-sequencing, and possibly cost overrun problems. I would suggest either including some construction management services in your architect's scope of work, or hiring a general contractor to handle the coordination and work sequencing on the project. Most architects will not want to assume these responsibilities, as they likely will not have time to manage subcontractors on a daily basis. On the other hand, hiring a general contractor to handle these issues will be an added expense. It may be money well spent, however, as it should save the headaches of project management, and quite possibly your job as well.

—Answer by Darren Duzyk, Sullivan & Duzyk, Lexington, Kentucky

A. How much time you should be physically present during your project depends on the nature of the work and the amount of daily progress. Your ability to inspect the work effectively should be the controlling factor—not time.

In terms of legal problems, you may face difficulties coordinating multiple subcontractors and multiple contracts.

—Answer by John P. Madden, Madden Mediation, New York, New York tors. As a result, he or she will already have a sense of who is reliable, who needs close attention, and who needs praise. As the homeowner, you won't know these things—but you'll have to learn them fast.

THE WORLD AT YOUR FINGERTIPS

• There are dozens of books on specific types of home renovation and do-it-yourself renovation. To browse the available titles, visit *www.amazon.com* and key in "home renovation" or "home remodeling."

• The DIY Network site includes information on acting as your own contractor. Go to *www.diynetwork.com/diy/home_ improvement* and click on "Be Your Own Contractor" in the left navigation bar.

REMEMBER THIS

• Keep in mind that your home renovation project will probably cost at least 20 percent more than you think it will.

• When you become your own contractor, you take on all the legal and financial responsibilities of a contractor.

• Never hire an unlicensed subcontractor.

• Never hire a subcontractor who does not have adequate insurance coverage.

• Know your limitations and your strengths.

CHAPTER 4

The Contractor

How to Choose a Good One

Bill and Carol were thinking about adding a porch to their house when they happened to drive by a storefront that advertised, "decks and porches built by pros." They went into the store and met the "pro," Mike, a new contractor in town. He came over to their house, made some suggestions that expanded on their original ideas, and drew some sketches for them. All was going well until Bill and Carol asked Mike for the names of homeowners with whom he had worked, what current renovations he was working on, and whether he could provide references. Mike hemmed and hawed, muttering about being new to the area; he claimed to have references out of state, if Bill and Carol wanted to talk with them. Bill and Carol declined, saying they needed time to think about hiring a contractor who didn't have work he could show them.

Selecting a contractor, like so many other decisions in the world of home renovation, tends to be a hit-or-miss affair—you might make a choice based on a recommendation from a friend, a sign posted in front of a house you like, or maybe just by combing through the yellow pages. Depending on how much effort you want to put into it, there are a number of things you can do to improve your chances of choosing the right contractor for your project.

This chapter outlines the steps you should take to select a contractor, and explains the significance of insurance and bonding. You'll also find some more general advice about how to communicate with your contractor. If you have a good relationship with your contractor, it's much more likely that you'll be able to anticipate extra costs and delays, and ultimately make your home renovation a success.

SELECTING A CONTRACTOR

Take the following five steps to identify the contractor who's right for your renovation:

Step One: Find Out as Much as You Can

It is extremely important that you speak with the people your contractor lists as references. Every contractor should provide several references; if not, you should find another contractor, as Bill and Carol did in the scenario above. And don't just call your contractor's references on the phone and talk with them; instead, invite yourself over for coffee. Look at the work your contractor did on their home, and find out how they enjoyed working with him or her. What was the scope of the work performed? Was their project similar to your project? Was the work done in accordance with their agreement? Was the work completed in the time frame that was proposed? Would they hire this contractor again? If not, why not? In addition, ask your contractor about other projects on which he or she is currently working. Get the names and addresses of homeowners the contractor is working for and talk with them, too.

It's also a good idea to talk to people in the home renovation community, such as plumbers, electricians, and interior designers; they usually know who the good contractors are. A local real estate agent can also be a good source, as he or she probably knows whose work has been an issue when a house is sold. Check out the Internet to see if your potential contractor has a website. Private agencies such as the Better Business Bureau may also be able to provide you with information about your contractor's reputation.

If you're satisfied with a contractor's reputation, double-check his or her credentials before signing a contract. Contact your state's licensing board to confirm that the contractor is licensed and bonded. Although not all states require that home contractors be licensed, those that do should have, at the very least, a record of each contractor's name and address, proof of the contractor's compliance with insurance laws, and a copy of his or her agreement to operate within the law. Some states require contractors to have a certain amount of experience and pass an exam in order to receive a license; others only require contractors to register their names and addresses. Having a state license doesn't mean the contractor will do a good job, but it's some assurance that he or she has made an effort to comply with the law. Talk to your city's building department; though they won't make any recommendations, many cities keep a list of licensed contractors.

Ask if your potential contractor belongs to a trade association, such as the Remodelers Council of the National Association of Home Builders, the National Association of the Remodeling Industry, or the National Kitchen & Bath Association. Many associations require a contractor to have been in business for a certain period of time, to have passed a credit check, and to have met all legal requirements imposed by his or her state. It wouldn't hurt to call the association to make sure the contractor's membership is current and to inquire about complaints. And check your secretary of state's business filings to determine whether the contractor is incorporated or registered in your state.

Finally, ask the contractor whom he or she will be using as subcontractors. Most contractors draw on a small pool of subcontractors they have used over the years. Some subcontractors run small businesses themselves (especially electricians and plumbers), so you can check out their reputations as well.

 THE UNLICENSED CONTRACTOR

In most states, any work costing over $500 in materials and labor must be completed by a licensed contractor. In addition, most cities require contractors and subcontractors to be licensed in order to acquire permits. This means that if, for some reason, you wanted to hire an unlicensed contractor, you would likely be doing renovation work without a permit. This is a nightmare scenario.

Don't let sentiment or friendship lead you to use an unlicensed contractor—it's nothing but trouble. There's no excuse for a contractor not having a license; it's not difficult for him or her to get one. Some states require applicants to pass a test, some states require only registration, and some states leave licensing to local governments. Whatever the requirements, a contractor who is unlicensed is someone who can't be bothered to study a little bit or fill out a few forms.

From the homeowner's financial and legal perspective, hiring an unlicensed contractor is rolling loaded dice. A contractor who does not have a license is probably not going to bother with liability insurance and workers' compensation, which means that the homeowner could be held liable if someone is injured during the project.

An unlicensed contractor could cause you serious problems down the line, even if you are satisfied with his or her work. If you have used an unlicensed contractor in the past, he or she probably didn't go through your city's building department, which means a permit wasn't issued and the work hasn't been inspected. So when you go to sell your home, the building department's records may not match the specifics of your house in terms of overall size, room location, and so on. If this is the case, and if an inspector thinks that unlicensed work has been done, you could be forced to open up walls, tear down structures, and redo the unlicensed work before your city will approve a certificate of occupancy—which is needed in most cities before a sale can take place.

From the contractor's perspective, it's important to realize that an unlicensed contractor has no legal standing and no right to receive payment for his or her work. That means that the unlicensed contractor doesn't even have the protection of the judicial system; without legal standing, the unlicensed contractor cannot use the courts to enforce a lien or even file a lawsuit. To be slightly melodramatic, an unlicensed contractor is an outlaw.

Step Two: Find Out if the Contractor Is Financially Stable

Residential construction companies tend to be small, family-run businesses. The contractor in these companies is usually someone who started with a hammer and a bag of nails and turned out to be good at construction—but that doesn't make the contractor a good businessperson. A financially unstable contractor can create all kinds of havoc for homeowners. Specifically, a contractor who goes broke during your project is likely to leave you with unpaid suppliers and subcontractors threatening to file liens against your home. To avoid these types of problems, it will be worth your time to ensure that your contractor is in good financial shape.

Information about contractors is available from many sources. Your state's licensing board should be able to tell you how long a contractor has been in business, and you can ask the contractor's suppliers about his or her payment history. If you have the nerve, you can also ask to see the contractor's bank statements and books. (Keep in mind that being bonded can provide you with important protections; for more information, see the section on bonding below.)

 THE CONTRACTOR'S LEGAL HISTORY

You can check court records to learn whether your contractor has been sued—or whether your contractor has sued customers, suppliers, or subcontractors. To see if any civil judgments or lawsuits are pending against the contractor, check with your local clerk of court. If someone sued the contractor over, say, poor workmanship, take that as a warning. Likewise, you might want to check with the nearest federal bankruptcy court to see whether this contractor has ever filed bankruptcy—a strong indication of financial instability.

Step Three: Get Three Bids

Take the time to get three separate bids for your project. You need to ensure that, when the work is done, you don't feel you could have completed it for thousands of dollars less than you paid. Before interviewing contractors, prepare a detailed plan of what you want accomplished. A contractor must have complete specifications for your project in order to prepare a realistic estimate of time, materials, and cost. And don't change the plan as you speak to different contractors; you need "apples to apples" quotations, in which each contractor is bidding on precisely the same job. If you don't outline the project in the exact same way to every contractor, then a contractor with a higher bid may be taking into account aspects of the project you did not make clear to the others.

If the contractors' bids are substantially different, then you need to look closely at the estimates to see where the bids diverge. There are two variables that determine the cost of each project. The first is **core work**, which is work on the walls, floors, ceilings, and everything that's behind those surfaces. The second is **finish work**, which is work on moldings, trim, marble, tile, and cabinetry. The costs associated with core work should be similar from contractor to contractor. On the other hand, the quality of the workmanship associated with finish work generally differs between contractors, causing their costs to diverge. If differences in the quality of finish work don't seem to account for cost differences between bids, then you need to ask questions—and get answers.

Suppose you solicit bids from three separate contractors. If the second contractor proposes spending 25 percent more on materials than the first, and the third proposes spending 25 percent less than the first, then you need to account for that discrepancy. Keep asking questions until you're satisfied with the answers. If one contractor's explanation doesn't make sense, look for another contractor. If you receive one bid for the job that's 50 percent higher than all the others, then you have to wonder if all your potential contractors have the same under-

TALKING TO A LAWYER

Q. We have selected a contractor to build a major addition to our house. He's a nice guy and has a good reputation, but we're running into problems with him because he resists putting things in writing. He offered us a bare-bones contract that seemed fair, but it doesn't cover a lot of the issues that we think a contract should cover. Are we wrong to demand that everything be in writing?

A. You're absolutely correct. Demand everything in writing.

—Answer by R. Stephen Hansell, lawyer, patent attorney, and construction arbitrator, Florence, Montana

standing of the job. Is there something wrong with your presentation of the project? Is the highest-bidding contractor approaching the job differently than the others—or is he or she simply charging more for everything?

Step Four: Does the Contractor Offer a Warranty and Carry Insurance?

Insurance is essential. Your contractor must have workers' compensation insurance and general liability insurance. If he or she doesn't, then you should start looking for another contractor. (See the discussion below for more information on this subject.)

In addition, ask whether the contractor provides a warranty on his or her work and on the materials—and make sure that any such warranty is mentioned in the contract. (Some contractors also offer extended warranties for an additional fee.)

Even if your contract doesn't specifically provide for a warranty, most courts recognize an **implied warranty of good workmanship** that will provide you with some protection. If the contractor is unqualified or does a bad job, then you can bring a lawsuit for breach of this implied warranty.

Step Five: Follow Your Instincts

Pay attention to the way contractors talk to you and whether they listen to you. Then trust your judgment. After all, the contractor is on his or her best behavior during the selling phase of the project. Any negative traits you notice before the work begins are probably going to be magnified after the work has started.

If a contractor starts talking to you about problems he or she is having with other homeowners, it's a good bet that he or she will soon be complaining to other people about *you*. Good contractors, if they talk at all about other homeowners, will talk in positive terms—about the good relationships they've had and the exciting work they've done. All good contractors sometimes have problems with homeowners, but they accept such problems as part of the job. Contractors who focus on their difficulties with customers are, at the very least, contractors who don't know how to deal with problems professionally. At the worst, they are contractors who create problems themselves.

 THE RIGHT OF RESCISSION

Federal law gives you, the purchaser, a three-day grace period within which you may change your mind and cancel a contract after you've signed it. If a contractor does not inform you of this right of rescission when you sign a contract, that contractor is violating the law. In addition, if a contractor fails to tell you about your right of rescission, you have up to three years to cancel the contract. Chapter 1 contains more information about this right.

If your contractor "forgets" to tell you about your right of rescission, he or she is probably not a legitimate businessperson. Cancel the contract in writing and start looking for another contractor.

INSURANCE

The ways in which a worker can get injured while working on your renovation are countless—pipes falling through floors, boards falling down, scaffolds collapsing, things simply falling and breaking, and so on. So when you hire a general contractor, you must require the contractor and subcontractors to carry two kinds of insurance:

1. Workers' compensation insurance; and
2. General liability insurance.

When you make the decision to hire a contractor, ask for a copy of his or her current workers' compensation and general liability certificates of insurance. If the contractor doesn't have both, you should walk away and find a contractor who does.

The insurance certificates should indicate:

• Effective dates of coverage—in other words, whether the insurance is current;

• The name of the insurance company;

• The name of the insurance agent;

• The amount of coverage purchased; and

• The names of insured parties. (Make sure the contractor is named as an insured party.)

Workers' compensation insurance provides coverage to the contractor and his employees in the event of job-related injuries. It is required by most states. Workers' compensation laws guarantee that employees who are injured on the job receive fixed monetary awards, without requiring any proof of negligence or fault. This means that a worker can seek workers' compensation whether the workplace is safe or unsafe, and even if the worker was injured as a result of his or her own mistake or fault.

If the workplace is reasonably safe, then an injured worker will only be able to seek workers' compensation, and will probably not be able to sue the employer for negligence. However, if the workplace is unsafe, then an injured employee may also be

able to make a negligence claim. To avoid the possibility of negligence suits (as well as for reasons of common sense and basic
human decency), contractors must provide reasonably safe work
sites for their workers. This includes the legal duty to warn workers of any defects or hazards at the site. Typically, a contractor
also has a duty to make sure that work is being performed safely,
that the workers are competent, and that the workers are com-
plying with safety regulations.

General liability insurance covers negligence that results
in property damage or bodily injury to someone other than the
contractor and the subcontractors. This insurance covers injury
to you and your family members, and to any friends and neighbors who might visit the premises while the renovation is going
on. As is the case with workers' compensation, it is standard for
general contractors to provide general liability coverage—so
avoid any contractor who doesn't.

Both of these forms of insurance cover the policyholder—in
this case, the contractor—because the contractor is the first person to be found liable if something goes wrong. However, the
place where the work is being performed belongs to you. This
means that if the contractor doesn't carry appropriate insurance,
the injured person is likely to sue you as well. Injured workers or
other people injured in your home may sue you personally for
providing a negligent workplace, and may also seek to recover
through your homeowner's insurance. The bottom line? Any
contractor who doesn't provide workers' compensation and general liability insurance is unwise—but any homeowner who allows that contractor on his or her property is equally unwise.

Even if your contractor has all the right insurance, you may
still be liable in the unlikely event that someone is injured on
your property, if the injury is caused by a dangerous condition
that you as the owner knew or should have known about. This
is a principle of personal injury law that applies all the time—
whether you are renovating, or just inviting friends into your
house for a Christmas party. So before the work starts, take a
minute to look around your house—at least in those areas
where the workers will be working and through which they'll be

ENSURE YOU INSURE

Here's another warning about unlicensed contractors. As a homeowner, you have an insurance policy that protects you if a guest is injured in your home. But if you employ someone in your home, and that person is injured, your homeowner's policy generally will not cover the potential liability. So, if you bring in unlicensed workers, you may find yourself uninsured, unless you obtain a separate workers' compensation policy.

walking—and check for hazards such as slippery surfaces, exposed nails, and loose stairs. As for your personal liability, your homeowner's insurance policy may cover you during a renovation project—but check your policy to be sure.

Depending on the type of renovation you have planned, your general contractor may also need to provide a builder's risk policy. Though such policies can also be written to cover special circumstances, they generally cover physical damage directly caused by the contractor (or subcontractor) to new or existing property, and to uninstalled appliances, cabinets, carpet, and other items related to the renovation. They can also cover indirect damage caused by delays in completion. Builder's risk policies typically exclude damages caused by natural occurrences, such as earthquakes and floods, and many policies also exclude damages from collapse caused by design or construction errors.

SURETY BONDS

Bonds are guarantees that a contractor will pay his or her subcontractors and complete the job. Bonding is an important aspect of multimillion-dollar construction projects, and is required on virtually all projects involving public construction. Though they do provide good protection for homeowners, bonds are used less frequently in cases of residential renovation.

BONDS

Be aware that the word "bond" can have two meanings. **Fully insured and bonded** generally means that a contractor has insurance coverage to protect against employee theft, vandalism, or negligence. If you have valuables in your home, ask to see a certificate or letter certifying that your contractor carries such a policy. A **surety bond**, on the other hand, is an insurance company's assurance that a contractor will complete his or her contract.

A **surety bond** is an agreement in which a surety company, typically a division of an insurance company, assures a homeowner that a contractor will perform his or her contract. Surety bonds offer assurance that a contractor is capable of completing the contract on time, within budget, and according to specifications. Most importantly, if the contractor defaults, the surety company is obligated to fulfill the contract. There are three types of surety bonds in common use in the construction context:

- The **bid bond** provides financial assurance that a contractor's bid has been submitted in good faith, that the contractor will enter into the contract if the bid is accepted, and that the contractor will provide the required performance and payment bonds. If the contractor fails to honor the bid, or fails to provide performance or payment bonds, the surety company will be liable for the difference between your contractor's promised bid and the next-lowest bid you received for your project, up to the face amount of the bond. The bond is usually written at 5 percent to 20 percent of the contract price, meaning that the contractor generally must pay between 5 and 20 percent of the contract price if he or she fails to perform.
- The **performance bond** protects the owner from financial loss if the contractor fails to perform the contract. If the contractor defaults, the surety company will either complete the project or pay to have it completed up to the limits of the bond. Most

performance bonds are written at 100 percent of the contract, and increase with each **change order** (alteration to the contract), which means that the homeowner generally will be fully compensated for the contract price in the event of a default.

- The **payment bond** assures that the contractor will pay the subcontractors and materials suppliers. A payment bond is often issued with a performance bond at no additional charge. If unpaid subcontractors or suppliers file a lien against a property, the owner of that property can notify them of the payment bond. They can then seek payment from the surety company. Note, however, that if the surety company does not pay, the lien will stay on the record and a foreclosure action can be maintained.

A fourth type of bond, which is less common, is the **contract bond**. A contract bond guarantees both job completion and payment of all labor and materials suppliers. In general, a bonding company will not have to pay more than the face amount of a contract bond.

Contractors have to take out separate bonds for each job, so bonds usually are issued only for jobs of $25,000 or more. If you require that a contractor obtain a bond, the cost of the job will increase for you because the contractor will include the bond premium—which generally will range from 0.5 percent to 2 per-

 IF YOU'RE BONDED . . .

If a contractor defaults, the surety company may rebid the job for completion, hire another contractor to complete the job, give financial assistance to the contractor so the job can be completed, or simply pay the penalty to the homeowner. If the surety company takes over, unpaid subcontractors and suppliers may still file a lien against the property. To protect yourself when a new contractor is brought in to finish your job, make sure that subcontractors are aware of the new contractor, and find out whether the new contractor has been issued a new bond to complete the work.

cent of the contract amount—in the contract price. This can be an expensive proposition—up to 10 percent of the contract price in the case of a residential swimming pool project. The smaller the dollar amount of your contract, the greater the percentage of that amount you will pay as a premium.

A contractor who's been approved by a bonding company is a very good risk. For the homeowner, bonds provide a number of important protections:

1. Qualifying a contractor for a surety bond is a statement by the surety company that the contractor is in solid financial health and is capable of doing the work.

2. Though subcontractors and suppliers can still file mechanic's liens against a project when a payment bond is in place, they are much less likely to do so, because the surety company has provided a guarantee that they will be paid.

3. In order to issue a bond, the surety company may require personal or corporate indemnity from the contractor. This means that if the surety company must pay on the bond, then the contractor has to repay the surety company. As a result, the contractor is far less likely to abandon the project.

4. If the contractor defaults, the surety company will fulfill the contract.

If bonds offer so many important protections, then why aren't they used very often in residential renovations? Basically, surety companies and residential contractors are not interested in spending the money or expending the effort necessary to obtain surety bonds for relatively small projects.

From the surety company's perspective, providing a bond for such projects simply may not be worthwhile. In order to qualify for bonding, a contractor has to demonstrate to the surety company that he or she is financially stable and has the construction expertise to carry out the project. Smaller residential contractors may not be financially healthy enough to provide such assurances. Moreover, the premium a contractor pays for a surety contract is based, in large part, on the dollar value of the contract. For this reason, it may not be cost-effective for a surety company to spend time and money investigating a contractor for a smaller job—for example, a $50,000 job that will net a premium of only about $1,000. Ultimately, the same resources are better spent investigating a contractor working on a multimillion-dollar project, who will have to pay the surety company a much larger premium.

From the contractor's perspective, it may not be worth the time and effort to qualify for bonds when most homeowners don't insist on them. After all, the process of qualifying involves an extensive investigation by the surety into the contractor's financial situation and the contractor's ability to handle the project. The investigation process can take from several weeks to a couple of months.

Despite the reluctance of surety companies and contractors to use performance and payment bonds for smaller jobs, the fact remains that bonds can provide the protection you most need in a renovation project. If you insist on them, and understand that your costs will be higher for doing so, then a contractor with some business history ought to be able to find a surety company to supply a bond for your project.

CONTRACTOR'S LICENSE BONDS

In many states, contractors are required to have **contractor's license bonds**, usually in the amount of $10,000. Such a bond is not a guarantee of performance or competence, or of the contractor's financial responsibility. In fact, these bonds do not even guarantee payment to a particular homeowner. Rather, contractor's license bonds are intended to help compensate *any* homeowner who has been damaged by contractor nonperformance. In Arizona, for example, the money paid for contractor's licensing bonds goes to the Residential Contractors Recovery Fund, which can compensate a homeowner for up to $30,000 if a contractor has failed to complete his or her job properly. Keep in mind, however, that although funds like this exist to compensate homeowners for actual damage, they usually cannot cover the total cost of nonperformance for the many complaints received.

KEEPING COSTS DOWN

When planning your renovation project, a few simple strategies can help to keep costs down:

- Don't skimp on the architect; you want to be right the first time.
- Work with a lawyer to root out hidden costs written into contracts.
- Insist that the contractor pass along to you any trade discounts on materials—or buy the materials yourself.
- Compare payment alternatives—flat versus hourly payment schemes, for example—and negotiate the most reasonable system of payment.
- Do part of the project yourself, such as some disassembly, prep work, and cleanup.
- Many showrooms will let you shop if you're accompanied by a designer. Look into this option as a way to buy materials at trade discounts of up to 50 percent.
- Buy recycled materials. For some homeowners, such materials have a charm all their own. As an example, lumberyards often stock old doors and other parts.
- Keep existing components, such as cabinetry, that you may not love—but can live with for now.

And in other states, such as in New Mexico—where contractor's license bonds help pay fines levied by the state that contractors have failed to pay—the funds aren't intended to help homeowners at all.

CONTRACTOR SCAMS

Be careful out there: The home renovation industry is rife with crooks. The most vulnerable homeowners are the elderly and those whose homes have been damaged in natural disasters.

If someone comes to your door offering to renovate your house, fix your roof, or replace your stucco, then your trouble-sensing antennae should stand on end. There's nothing inherently illegal about traveling door-to-door soliciting business, but home renovation is one of those businesses that functions most smoothly on the basis of referrals from satisfied customers. Be wary of solicitors who eschew this system by going door-to-door seeking business. (These types of solicitations are common in places that have been affected by natural disasters, especially from roofers following a hurricane.) Your best bet is to steer clear of door-to-door contractors. They are liable to take your money, slap a few shingles on your roof, and leave town.

Various state agencies—including your local contractor's licensing board, attorneys general, and police—may be able to help you if you've been scammed. But attempting to recover the money you've lost can be a long, difficult, and often futile quest. This book has mentioned repeatedly that home renovation usually takes longer and costs more than you think it will, that you should plan to spend an additional 20 percent of your total budget on cost overruns, and so on. Anyone working a scam will likely offer you an opportunity to save a lot of time and money, but you have to accept that this simply isn't possible. Home renovation is not cheap; anyone who tells you it can be is probably scamming you.

In particular, be on the alert for three notorious scams:

The Furnace-Breaker Scam

Someone comes to your door claiming to be an inspector from a local government agency, and demands to check your furnace. He or she then tampers with the furnace, which otherwise was not in need of repair, then claims that he or she knows someone who can fix it—for a steep price.

Don't let anyone into your home whom you're not expecting. If somebody arrives on your doorstep unannounced, ask to see identification. If you're in doubt, ask for the phone number of the agency and call it. If you get an answering machine instead of a real person who can confirm your visitor's identity, close the door on the alleged "inspector" and call the police.

The Chimney Burn Scam

You respond to an advertisement for chimney cleaning at a price far below the going rate. However, the "discount" cleaner inevitably reports that your chimney needs a new liner or other major repair costing thousands of dollars.

Before you write a check, get a second opinion from a member of the National Chimney Sweep Guild or your state's guild.

The "I'm-Doing-Work-Down-the-Street-and-Have-Some-Leftovers" Scam

In this scam, a contractor or worker tells you that he or she has extra material left over from a recent job. If you act now, you're told, you can have the missing shingles on your roof fixed for a few hundred dollars, or your driveway resurfaced for next to nothing.

The reality, however, is that you just aren't that lucky. Any unsolicited construction work is likely to be trouble. The purveyors of these so-called bargains may take your money and not return, or they may do a quick-and-dirty job that will fall apart at the first sign of rain. Your chances of receiving quality work from workers using leftover materials are almost nil. Think about it: One of the most common complaints about contractors is that they are unresponsive—you can't get them to bid on your project, they stop work on your project to work on another one, and so on. As annoying as this problem may be, what it indicates is that good contractors—for all their faults—are busy. They don't have time to be driving around neighborhoods looking for roofs with loose shingles. Any contractor who does have that kind of time is *not* someone you want working on your home.

**WARNING SIGNS OF A
RENOVATION SCAM**

- You can't verify the name, address, telephone number, or credentials of the contractor.

- The contractor doesn't furnish references.

- You can't verify the license or insurance information of the contractor.

- Information you receive from the contractor is out of date.

- The contractor tries to pressure you into signing a contract.

- The contractor claims you will receive a discount or special low rate because your home will be used for advertising purposes.

- The contractor claims you will receive a special price—but only if you sign the contract today.

- The contractor solicits door-to-door.

- The contractor claims to have discounted materials left over from a previous job.

- The contractor offers you a discount in exchange for finding him or her other customers.

- The contractor offers you exceptionally lengthy guarantees.

- The contractor claims to work for a government agency.

- You are asked to pay for the entire job in advance.

- The contractor accepts cash payments only.

- The contractor asks you to acquire your own building permits.

- The contractor suggests you borrow money from a lender he or she knows.

- The contractor engages in bait-and-switch tactics. (An example: after luring you with an ad that offers an unbeatable deal, a contractor suddenly informs you that the materials needed for your job aren't available—but that he or she can give you a bargain on another, more-expensive job.)

- The contractor furnishes estimates that do not take into account delivery or installation costs.

- The contractor insists on starting work before you sign a contract.

- A salesperson tells you that you can't meet the general contractor until after you've signed a contract.

- The contractor fails to provide a right-of-rescission notice.

- The contractor discourages you from reading the contract thoroughly, or dismisses confusing language as standard boilerplate (i.e., "lawyer-speak").

ESTABLISHING A GOOD RELATIONSHIP WITH THE CONTRACTOR

After you've chosen a contractor, you should take some time to think about how you can build a good working relationship with him or her. First, think about what each of you hopes to accomplish. You, the homeowner, are spending perhaps tens of thousands of dollars to improve your home—which is not just the place where you live, but is also probably the most significant investment of your lifetime. On the other side of the equation is the contractor, who spends money for supplies and subcontractors, and who makes money by completing your job as efficiently and inexpensively as possible.

Now let's discuss some hard truths, because the more you understand about what you're getting into, what contractors really do, and the inevitability of certain problems, the better your chances are of getting what you want. Above all, remember: (1) your project will take longer than you think it will; and (2) it will also cost more.

Your project could take longer than you think for any number of reasons: because bad weather causes delays, because materials are in short supply, because materials arrive at the job site broken (or are not what the contractor ordered), because a brief delay at one stage of the project causes a longer delay later, and so forth. Construction is a business of timing, and a seemingly infinite number of things can go wrong and cause delays. For example, if you're renovating a bathroom and the manufacturer sends the wrong faucet, it could take three weeks for you to get the right one—and your job could suddenly be three weeks behind schedule.

Your project will probably cost more than you think it will because homeowners almost always change their minds. There is no such thing as a construction project that doesn't undergo changes, and each change adds to the project's cost. If a change is made in plenty of time for the contractor to adjust the work, the added labor cost will be minimal; if the change is made after work has already begun, the result could be a massive increase in costs.

However, the fact that your project will take longer and cost more than you expect does not mean that it will be a total nightmare, or that you and the contractor will end up in court. If the homeowner and contractor talk to each other throughout a job; if the homeowner asks questions and raises concerns as they occur; if the contractor keeps the homeowner informed about the progress of the job and prepares the homeowner for bad news before it arises, then the renovation will probably be successful.

As a homeowner, there are several things you can do to make your renovation a success. First and foremost, be clear about what you want—even down to minor details, such as the sizes of handles and knobs on cabinet doors. At the same time, you have to be realistic; you have an image of what your finished renovation will look like, but you may not be willing or able to pay what it will cost to make that image a reality.

The contractor can also help to ensure that your job runs smoothly, in large part by communicating effectively. For one thing, the contractor must be clear and honest about what can be accomplished for the price the homeowner is paying. A contractor's costs are tied to time; he or she cannot afford to spend the same amount of time on a $25,000 job as on a $100,000 job. Likewise, if a homeowner wants $50,000 worth of work but is only paying $25,000, the contractor has to set the homeowner straight. Ultimately, the contractor must remember that the homeowner doesn't speak the language of construction—which means that he or she may not know what to ask for. Good communication is essential; it is up to both the homeowner and the contractor to make sure they understand each other.

In order to keep communication channels open, the relationship between the homeowner and contractor should be one of equals. You may be a novice when it comes to renovation, but you'll throw off the balance of the relationship if you expect your contractor to hold your hand. As the homeowner, you have to take responsibility for what's happening in and to your home. If you see something that doesn't look like you expected it to look, or if you can't figure out why the plumber is running the pipes

---

 TALK TO YOUR CONTRACTOR

When planning a renovation with your contractor, discuss work conditions. You need to know when the contractor plans to be on the job—both the hours each day that the workers will be in your home, and the days when the contractor will be there directly supervising them. You also should be clear about what you expect from the workers: whether they can smoke in your home, play radios, or work without shirts, and which bathroom they can use.

Make sure the contractor makes the loss of your vital living space as bearable as possible. If your kitchen is going to be out of commission, see if you can set up a refrigerator, microwave, and hot plate in another room. If a subcontractor is going to turn off the water or power for any length of time, insist on twenty-four-hours' notice.

Finally, talk about security. You will probably give the contractor a key; it would be a good idea to attach a lockbox to your house in which to store it. Make sure you know who has the combination.

---

north-south instead of east-west, you have to ask. Don't ever be too intimidated to speak up. You should follow your instincts. Remember: If something looks wrong to you while it's being built, it's still going to look wrong to you after it's been built and the contractor has long since left your home—and it will bug you every time you see it. So say something. The worst that can happen is that you'll learn why something is being done in a particular way.

See chapter 6 for information about some common problems that homeowners may encounter during the renovation process, including failure to start, delay, shoddy workmanship, and failure to complete a job.

MINIMIZE THE HASSLE

For the homeowner, a renovation project is the *only* project, the *only* priority; for the contractor, it's just another job. You are dealing with your home; you are going to be there every day. For most contractors, on the other hand, the goal is to get in and out with the least possible amount of hassle.

Working with a contractor is an intimate thing, because the home is an intimate space. The contractor and subcontractors will get to know you, they will get to know your children and your pets, they will see how neatly you keep your house, they will hear you snap at your kids, and they will hear you on the phone.

Keeping all this in mind, do what you can to make the relationship as anxiety-free as possible.

THE WORLD AT YOUR FINGERTIPS

• The National Association of the Remodeling Industry, at *www.nari.org*, has lists of certified home renovation contractors, broken down by zip code. The National Kitchen & Bath Association, at *www.nkba.org*, also provides lists of contractors.

- The Contractors State License Board of California is an excellent resource for information about contractors. Visit *www.cslb.ca.gov/consumers/beforehiring.asp*.
- The Arizona Registrar of Contractors has created a good checklist for homeowners seeking to hire a licensed contractor. Visit *www.rc.state.az.us/Acrobat/Misc/HiringContractor.pdf*.

REMEMBER THIS

- Selecting the right contractor is the most important piece of the home renovation puzzle. Get at least three bids from different contractors before you begin.
- Before hiring a contractor, ask for copies of his or her workers' compensation and general liability certificates of insurance. If the contractor doesn't have both of these kinds of insurance, you should walk away and find a contractor who does.
- If you've hired a contractor to do a large, expensive job, look into the cost of a surety bond. A contractor who's been approved by a bonding company is a very good risk—and if things go wrong, you're covered.
- You and the contractor must talk about your project on a continuing basis. The more the two of you communicate, the fewer problems you will have.
- Good contractors don't solicit door-to-door.

CHAPTER 5

Get It in Writing

Your Contract with the Contractor

Ben and Jane had spent several hours going over their plans for a new kitchen with Paul, the contractor they had selected to do the work. Now was the time to put everything down on paper—to formalize their agreement with a contract. When Ben and Jane arrived at Paul's office, he handed them a simple one-page statement indicating the costs of the various aspects of the project, the starting date, and his commitment to complete the project before the start of the new year. When Ben and Jane complained to Paul about the lack of specifics in the contract, he shrugged and said, "This is our standard contract; we've never had any problems with it." The two homeowners were a little nervous, but they had spent so much time preparing for the project and choosing a contractor that they just wanted to get the new kitchen started . . . so they signed.

Home renovation can be, and usually is, a pretty casual affair. If you stop to think about it, however, a casual approach to renovation can be a little dicey. After all, you're turning over thousands of dollars to a bunch of strangers who will walk through your house with hammers and saws and wallboard and lumber, knocking down walls, ripping up pipes, and making entire portions of your house off-limits for months at a time.

But you want to have a new bedroom built, or a bathroom expanded, so you call around to your relatives and friends and get some names of contractors, and you call contractors until a couple of them actually show up to talk to you about the job. They do a little measuring, tap on some walls, draw a little sketch, and come back with a quote. Then you sit down to finalize details and sign a contract that the contractor has drawn up.

In the hands of a skilled, honest contractor, and with a little luck, the project will be completed with no major problems, and you'll be glad you did it. But things rarely go smoothly. You might change your mind about some details, the contractor might disappear for a week, the plumber could drop a pipe through the floor, or the vanity that gets delivered may not be the one you ordered.

If you experience these kinds of setbacks or have a dispute with your contractor, the contract you've signed will be your first stop for resolving the problem. If the contract has been properly drafted, it will tell you who is responsible for what problems, what steps you can take, and how disputes can be resolved if you can't work things out.

This chapter covers the basics of a good contract, and explains in brief the provisions that yours should include.

CONTRACT BASICS

The best way to protect yourself in the context of home renovation is to have a good written contract with the contractor. Contracts serve two purposes: to set out the agreement, and to state what happens when things go wrong or if circumstances change. In the case of home renovation, the contract should specify the details of the job—whether it entails putting a new roof on your house, building a swimming pool in your backyard, or turning that little bathroom next to the hall closet into a big bathroom with new plumbing. The contract should specify the amount that you, the homeowner, agree to pay the contractor upon completion of the job. The contract should also include enforcement mechanisms—for example, a provision stating that if the new roof leaks, the contractor must fix it in ten days; or that if you, the homeowner, fail to make a payment, the work stops. That's why you have a contract: not for the easy times, but for the rough times—for the mistakes and the disagreements.

A contract, whether written or oral, spells out the agreement for both sides. Ultimately—and this is the way lawyers approach contracts—if you wind up in court with your contractor, the contract tells the court what the parties agreed, and the court will hold you and the contractor to that agreement. But if the contract omits an important detail, how can the court decide what that detail should have been? For example, if your contract omits the start date of your project, how can the court tell when the project was supposed to start? You and the contractor might have reached an understanding, but if that understanding isn't reflected in the contract, the court can't enforce it. (Of course, reasonableness does enter into the discussion. So if you signed a contract in February that didn't specify a start date, and the contractor still hasn't started work by December, a court is likely to find the contractor's behavior unreasonable. But what if it were only May instead of December? Would the court still find this unreasonable?)

 BE PREPARED

In order to be as clear as possible, and to get exactly what you want, be prepared. Take some time to decide what you want, how much you are willing to pay for it, and what you need to do to protect yourself. You also have to know ahead of time what details your contractor will want included in the contract, and why. And—this is very important—you have to be prepared to walk away from the contractor if you are not totally comfortable with the contract.

If you're not sure of yourself, then the contractor—who has been through this process many more times than you have—will recognize that you don't really know what you're doing, and will take charge and dictate the terms.

When you're preparing to negotiate, think leverage. The contractor's leverage is his or her ability to do the work; once the workers march into your house, you are at the contractor's mercy. Your leverage is money; the contractor wants to make sure he or she gets paid. Remember: the contractor wants to do the job (and get paid for doing it) as much as you want to have the job done.

NEGOTIATING THE CONTRACT

When you and the contractor agree on the terms of the project, the contractor will present you with a "standard" contract—often a preprinted form. The contract your contractor slides across the table probably has not been written with your best interests in mind. However, this is strictly a matter of business; there's nothing dishonest or even shady about it. Contracts are about protection and leverage, and the person who writes the contract is going to give himself or herself all the protection and all the leverage the law allows—which is plenty. The contractor's contract will invariably provide him or her with 100 percent protection and, depending on the scruples of the contractor, may be seeded with traps for the unwary homeowner.

In fact, there is no such thing as a "standard" contract. Every contract is subject to negotiation, and any contract can be changed, annotated, or rewritten. If a person flat out refuses to negotiate a contract, you may want to seriously consider walking away from the deal.

You have to understand what protection you need in the contract and what leverage you can build into it, so don't sign it right away. Take it home, read through it very carefully, and think about where you will stand once you sign. What has the contractor promised, and what have you promised? The best negotiating stance to take is that you want the project to go well, and the best way to accomplish that is for everything in the contract to be as clear as possible. By "everything," we mean the work to be done, the timing, the cost, and who's responsible for what. The more vagueness there is in the contract, the less understanding there is between you and the contractor, and the greater the likelihood that the project will run off the rails. The more certain you are as to what you can expect from the contractor, and how much the project will actually cost, the less anxiety there will be for you. And if the contractor realizes that you're going to pay attention to the work, he or she will do a better job.

CHANGING THE CONTRACT

To change a contract as a result of negotiation, simply cross out language to which you don't agree, and annotate the terms that you wish to change. You can also add a **rider** (an additional provision or clause, sometimes written on a separate page). Make sure both parties initial and date any changes.

At the contract stage, especially where tens of thousands of dollars are at stake, spending a few hundred dollars on a lawyer can be a smart investment. If you have questions, a construction or real estate lawyer can answer them. A lawyer can also help you clarify your thinking about the terms to which you will agree, and the terms that you want to negotiate. Chapter 9 provides more information on finding and working with a lawyer.

ORAL CONTRACTS

Let's talk about oral contracts, which are spoken agreements that have not been finalized in writing. In most states, oral contracts are valid contracts—but they're a bad idea, period. Don't rely on them. Instead, get your agreement in writing. Don't start your project with an oral contract, and if you have a written contract for a project that's already underway, don't make any additional agreements orally.

There are several compelling legal reasons to avoid oral contracts. The first is that some states still rigidly enforce the **Statute of Frauds**, an old common-law rule that any agreement relating to interests in real property, and any contract in excess of a certain (usually small) amount, must be in writing. If it's not in writing, the courts won't even need to decide who's right; the contract is simply invalid. If your state forbids oral contracts involving real property, you will be unable to enforce such a contract, because it will be legally invalid. (Note that in some states, such as California, the contractor licensing board requires the contractor to have contracts in writing. Under these circumstances, a complaint to the state board may get you some assistance, because the contractor is in the wrong for not having a written contract with you.)

The second legal reason for avoiding oral contracts involves the **parol evidence rule**, which says (roughly) that a written agreement signed by two parties constitutes the *entire* agreement between the parties—and no outside behavior can change that written agreement. If you and your contractor make an oral change to your written agreement, the parol evidence rule will apply if problems arise. Any oral agreements you reach will not be considered part of your contract if you haven't put them in writing.

The third reason to avoid oral contracts is a matter of evidence. With a written contract, proof of the terms of your agreement is right there, on paper. With an oral contract, the only proof of the agreement is what you remember—and that may differ from what the contractor remembers. Even honest people can have different understandings of what was agreed regarding cost, the types of materials to be used, or how change orders would be handled. It's not impossible to prove that your recollection of old conversations—some of which may have taken place months or even years ago—is better than the other side's, but it's very difficult.

The fourth issue is a practical one. It is very unlikely that someone making an oral contract is going to discuss all the issues a contract needs to cover, such as mechanic's lien issues, workers' compensation coverage, or warranties. Contractual coverage of these issues is vital to the protection of the homeowner, and an oral contract simply won't cover them. If you are serious about renovating your home—and about spending what may amount to thousands of dollars doing so—you won't risk your own legal protection by making an oral contract.

( ) TALKING TO A LAWYER

Q. I made an oral agreement with a contractor for a number of small renovations to my house. The contractor continually delayed the work, and he misled me into thinking that some additional work was included in the original price, which it wasn't. I have paid the subcontractors for some of this extra work, assuming the original price would be adjusted accordingly. I have now received a bill from the contractor that doesn't take into account any of my payments to the subcontractors. Not only that, but some of the original work has not been completed. Because none of this was in writing, where do I stand?

A. There are a couple of issues here: the potential fraud committed by your contractor, the direct payments you made to the subcontractors, and the fact that the agreed-upon work has not been completed.

More than likely, you can make a breach-of-contract claim based on the difference between the work performed and the work you understand the contractor to have promised. If the contractor intentionally led you to believe that certain work was included in the contract price, but then requested extra compensation for it, you may also have the basis for a fraud claim. Even if you don't actually make such a claim, the threat of a potential fraud claim may be a valuable bargaining chip as you attempt to resolve this matter with the contractor.

If the oral contract was silent on the issue of direct payment to subcontractors for additional work, you may well have been within your rights to pay them directly. However, the contractor may still have a valid claim against you for overhead and profit from the subcontractor's work—markup—if he had to manage or coordinate that work. The outcome will depend on the parties' agreement regarding additional work—and on who those parties are.

As for the agreed-upon work that remains uncompleted, you appear to have a clear breach-of-contract claim based upon the contractor's nonperformance. I would suggest not paying him until, at a minimum, he completes the agreed-upon work.

—Answer by Darren Duzyk, Sullivan & Duzyk,
Lexington, Kentucky

WHAT TO INCLUDE

What follows is a list and brief description of the issues you'll need to address in your contract in order to protect yourself. Addressing these issues before they arise is your protection against loss of time and money. If you do things right, a contract can also protect you from losing your home.

You're entitled to address these issues in the contract, and you should make sure that you do so. Though there will naturally be some back-and-forth in your negotiation of your contract with the contractor, the bargaining process isn't a trade-off. Thus, a contractor convincing you to give up your valuable rights—"Okay, I'll supply a certificate of insurance if you agree that change orders can be oral"—is not acceptable. Including terms that address the issues detailed below should not interfere with the contractor's ability to do the work or to get paid fairly for it. Instead, addressing these issues will force the contractor to be on the ball and to pay attention to your project—and if that's too much of a burden . . . well, that's probably not the contractor you want knocking down your walls.

As you examine this list, remember that the two main purposes of the contract are to define exactly what the job is and to protect yourself if the job goes sour. Don't shrug off any of these

---

 BREACH AND MATERIAL BREACH

A person is said to **breach** a contract if they break a promise that they agreed to in the contract. A **material breach** occurs when one party's breach is serious enough to injure the other party in some way. Many contracts identify what specific acts will constitute material breaches of the contract. If there has been a material breach of the contract by one party, the other party can terminate the contract, and pursue a legal action for breach of contract.

issues as petty concerns, and don't let the contractor shrug them off as unnecessary or burdensome. If the contractor resists addressing any of these issues, find a new contractor.

We'll have more to say about each issue later in this book; for now, we'll just provide brief explanations.

Mechanic's Liens

We start with **mechanic's liens** (called **construction liens** in some states) because, of all the issues discussed in this section, issues relating to mechanic's liens can present the greatest danger to homeowners. In some circumstances, an unpaid mechanic's lien can lead to foreclosure on your home.

Any person or business providing services, labor, or materials for work performed on real property is entitled to record a lien against that property if they are not paid for the work or materials. A **lien** is a claim for money that attaches to the property. When a lien is recorded, a claim for the amount owed is placed on record with the county title office. As a result, you won't be able to borrow money against your property or sell the property without paying the claim. The lien will also affect your credit rating. Worst of all, if the lien is not paid, in many states the **lienholder** (the contractor or subcontractor) can force you to sell the property to satisfy the lien. Just about anyone who has been involved in your project can record a lien against your property if they are not paid, including the contractor, the subcontractors, the architect, and any company that supplied materials.

At a minimum, if a lien is placed against your home, you will have to pay the debt that is the basis for the lien, or retain a lawyer to negotiate the lien or fight it in court. If a person or business has done the work (or supplied materials) and has not been paid, then you will very likely have to pay—even if you've already paid someone else for the same work. Pay twice for the same work? That's right: If you've paid your contractor for work, but he or she hasn't paid the subcontractor, you might be responsible for paying the subcontractor as well.

How can you avoid this situation? First order of business:

LIEN WAIVERS

A lien waiver from the contractor, and his or her assurance that everyone else has been paid, is not good enough. You have to know that the subcontractors and suppliers for your project have also been paid. A lien waiver from each subcontractor and supplier is the only way to be sure.

When you're negotiating your contract with the contractor, ensure that the contractor's lien rights are waived as you make periodic payments. Here's how to do it: When you make a payment, insist that the contractor provide you with statements from himself or herself, from all the subcontractors working on your project, and from all the materials suppliers for your project. These statements should indicate that the parties have been paid for the work they have completed up to that point (or for the supplies they have provided), and that they waive their rights to file a lien against you for that completed portion of the work. At the end of the project, procure a full release of lien rights (called a **lien waiver**) from everyone involved in the project before making the final payment. Chapter 7, "Resolving Disputes," includes more information about liens.

Warranties

You should also ensure that the contract contains **warranties** (guarantees) that the work has been completed in a "workmanlike" manner, and that the materials used are guaranteed to last for a certain number of years. Most reputable contractors will guarantee their work for one year; materials are typically guaranteed against defects for several years. In addition to the seller's warranty, a standard manufacturer's warranty usually covers materials. Under this warranty, the manufacturer will probably cover replacement of defective parts, but not the labor costs of replacement. Sellers' warranties, whether provided by local companies or giant home stores, typically cover labor costs as well as parts.

And don't forget the subcontractors: They need to sign warranties on their work, too. If the project, or your home, falls apart, you'll want to hold liable everyone who was responsible, and a warranty gives subcontractors less room to maneuver. Which brings up another point: Requiring everyone to provide warranties on their work puts them on notice that you're keeping a serious eye on the project, which can only help bring about a successful and happy ending.

For purposes of a warranty, what constitutes "workmanlike" completion of work? Every industry has its own standards as to what constitutes good work and what falls short. In the construction industry there are generally accepted ways of building things, and every municipality has a building code. Municipal building codes are very specific about how construction must be done—how many beams are required to support a floor, the size of the beams, how thick the stucco on a wall should be, and so on—and they serve as an objective measure of what is "workmanlike." If a contractor does not build up to code, then his work is quite obviously not "workmanlike" for purposes of satisfying a warranty.

Cost

Although it sounds obvious, this point can't be overstated: Your contract has to make clear how much the project is going to cost.

Some contractors will offer to complete your project based on an estimate of its final cost, then will calculate the actual cost of the project on an hourly basis. Others will offer to complete the project on a **cost-plus basis**, which means that the contractor gets paid his or her costs plus a percentage, which he or she determines, as profit. As you can imagine, a contract that pays the contractor by the hour or on a cost-plus basis provides the contractor with all the leverage. He or she has no incentive to hold down costs or to cap his or her profits. Don't allow this. If

NAIL DOWN YOUR COSTS

Most home renovation projects end up costing more and taking longer than homeowners anticipate. The more precisely you outline costs in your contract before your project begins, the less likely you are to experience runaway costs and lengthy delays once the project is underway.

you can't tell simply by reading your contract exactly how much your project is going to cost, you don't have a good contract.

The contract should clearly state the costs of labor and materials. An experienced contractor will have a good idea of how much work is required, what materials are needed, and how much time the project will take. Moreover, the contract should break down costs into clear categories: labor and materials for plumbing, labor and materials for carpentry, and so on. This will allow you to ask appropriate questions if your project appears to be running over budget—for example, why what appeared to be a simple plumbing job is costing so much.

Since a lot of renovation projects begin before final decisions have been made about certain details, such as fixtures, your contract needs to outline a clear process for ironing out such details and their costs.

The contractor will probably want to include a clause addressing the costs of unanticipated problems. This is fair, but make sure you discuss what sorts of problems might occur, and what will happen if they do. For example, if a contractor is installing new plumbing in your old house, and his estimate is based on the assumption that the joists under your bathroom floor run from east to west, that assumption should be stated in the contract. If it turns out that the joists actually run from north to south, your contract should clearly indicate the sorts of problems that may result, as well as the solutions to those problems and their costs. Of course, the solutions and costs detailed in your contract will be approximate, but the contract can nonetheless provide you with a good general idea of what to expect.

Payment Structure

You will want to spread out payments over the course of your project. Typically, this means making periodic payments at certain milestones in the work—for example, upon completion of plasterboard taping, installation of ceramic tile, and so on. Final payment should not be due until all the work is completed and you have procured releases from liens from *all* of the necessary parties.

Do not accept a lump-sum payment schedule. Just as your contractor will be unwilling to wait until the project is completed to receive payment, you shouldn't have to pay the entire amount due before work starts. You and the contractor both need to have bargaining leverage in case something goes wrong during the course of your project. If you pay for everything up front, you'll lose valuable leverage; the only leverage you'll have will come from the threat of a lawsuit for breach of contract—which will be time-consuming and expensive, and won't get that new bathroom built.

 A WORD OF CAUTION ABOUT DOWN PAYMENTS

Many states impose caps on the allowable value of down payments for renovation projects. In California, for instance, a down payment cannot exceed $1,000 or 10 percent of the total price for the applicable project, whichever is less. For swimming pool projects in California, the maximum down payment is $200 or 2 percent of the total project price, whichever is less. Check with your state contractor's licensing board before making a down payment. (Most state boards have websites.)

Change Orders

Probably the most common legitimate reason for an increase in the cost of a renovation is the homeowner's change of mind after the project has begun. A **change order** is an order for the contractor to change something that was agreed upon, or at least understood, at an earlier time—anything from the placement of lighting or routing of plumbing to the size or shape of a room— and can originate with either the homeowner or contractor. For example, the contractor might initiate a change order if he or she runs into an unanticipated problem. Change orders can dramatically increase the cost of your project.

As a homeowner, your contract should specify that any change orders must be in writing and signed and approved by you before the work detailed in the order can begin. Written change orders should include descriptions of the work to be done and its cost; if you and the contractor disagree about the cost of a change, it's better to have that disagreement before the contractor has purchased additional materials and refocused his subcontractors. If you don't include this requirement in your contract and you disagree with your contractor after the work has been completed, there's really nothing you can do about it— and you'll have to pay for the work.

Start Date and Completion Date

In your contract, set a start date and a completion date for your renovation. Once again, use the contract to establish certainty. Set a start date, and provide for a financial penalty if the contractor doesn't start the project on that date. For example, include a clause that reads, "the homeowner has the right to deduct one thousand dollars from the final cost if the contractor fails to start on time." Do the same with your project's completion date; if you don't, the project might last for months beyond its expected completion time. For example, you could specify in your contract that you are entitled to deduct a certain dollar amount from the project's final cost for each week that work continues past the agreed-upon date. At the very least, such a clause will encourage your contractor to set reasonable dates instead of overly optimistic ones.

The bane of all home renovation jobs, successful or not, is the contractor's universal habit of running from job to job—which means that some homeowner, somewhere, is being left in the lurch for an hour, a day, or even a week. Use your contract to ensure that you don't become one of these unlucky homeowners. Build a **diligence requirement** into your contract, which provides that once the contractor starts the project, he or she must proceed diligently to its finish. What does "diligence" mean in this context? As long as the other side agrees, it can mean whatever you want it to mean. For example, your contract could specify that if there is no activity on your project for a certain amount of time—two days, a week, or whatever amount of time you think makes sense—then you have the right to deduct a specified amount from the project's final cost. The contract could further provide that a lack of activity on your project for a certain amount of time means that your contractor is in breach of the contract. You don't want to be in the position of having to file a lawsuit when your kitchen and bathroom are torn up, but you do want the possibility of filing such a lawsuit as leverage in your dealings with the contractor. That leverage can help to make your project the one your contractor is running *to*, not *from*.

Insurance

As discussed in chapter 4, insurance is an absolute necessity. Demand a certificate of insurance from the contractor and subcontractors certifying that they have workers' compensation coverage. It is extremely important that you receive copies of all relevant certificates of insurance. If the contractor or subcontractors don't have workers' compensation coverage, then you can be held liable for on-the-job injuries that occur at your house.

Your contractor will also need to provide proof of liability coverage. If the contractor damages your house, you want his or her insurance rates to increase—not the premiums on your homeowner's insurance. More seriously, if anyone is harmed during the course of your project—for example, the kid next door who wanders onto the job site—and the contractor does not have insurance, the injured party could look to your home-owner's insurance for compensation.

Your contract should also include a **waiver of subrogation** for damages caused by the contractor to third parties. These waivers provide that if the contractor is found liable for negligently injuring someone—for example, that kid next door—the contractor cannot turn around and sue you for reimbursement of the damages paid. To give yourself added protection, you should also include an **indemnity provision** in the contract, which requires the contractor to indemnify (reimburse) you in the event that you are found liable for any injuries occurring during the renovation. This means that the contractor would be required to reimburse you for whatever amount you had to pay to an injured person.

Description of the Work to Be Done

Here's another obvious point: Your contract should include a detailed description of the work to be performed. It's not enough simply to say, for example, "Contractor agrees to redo kitchen." As a lawyer would say: "Define redo." Make explicit the scope of the work—and if it's anything other than a minor project, include the work order and drawings of the work to be performed. Before you sign the contract, take the drawings and work order to an **architect** or another contractor, and get his or her appraisal of whether the contract is sufficiently detailed and whether the specifications match the proposed work.

Responsibility for Permits and Arranging for Inspections

Every contract should state that the contractor is responsible for acquiring the necessary building permits. No matter where you live, you will need them. (As an exception, many cities do not re-

TALKING TO A LAWYER

Q. *One condition in our contract is that the contractor will be on-site to manage all subcontractor work. So far, each time the subcontractors have been here, the contractor has been absent. This has necessitated my wife's management of the subcontractors, a job for which she doesn't have the time or expertise. We have told the contractor that this is unacceptable, but he still doesn't show up to supervise. Is this a material breach? If it isn't, when does it become one?*

A. Your contractor's behavior appears to constitute a material breach, since your contract clearly states that he is to be physically present during all subcontractors' work. Any ambiguity in the contract should be construed against the drafter—presumably, in your case, the contractor. The fact that it may be difficult for your contractor to determine when subcontractors will be on-site is his problem—not yours.

> —Answer by R. Stephen Hansell, lawyer, patent attorney, and construction arbitrator, Florence, Montana

A. Whether the contractor's failure to manage the subs on-site constitutes a material breach will likely depend upon the scope of the work each party has been performing. For example, if subcontractors are performing 90 percent of the work on your project, the contractor's behavior may well constitute a material breach. Conversely, if the general contractor is performing most of the work and the subs are working on less complex aspects of the project, his behavior is not likely to constitute a material breach. In any event, because of the time your wife has spent performing the contractor's duties as set forth in the contract, you may have a pretty firm basis for deducting some portion of his fees from the project price.

> —Answer by Darren Duzyk, Sullivan & Duzyk, Lexington, Kentucky

NOTICE TO CURE

In the last several years, many states have passed laws requiring homeowners to give contractors "notice to cure" construction defects before the homeowners can file lawsuits. If you live in one of these states, this means that you must give your contractor a chance to fix any problems with your renovation before you can sue.

The statutes generally allow a certain amount of time for the homeowner to provide the contractor with written notice of the defective work (typically forty-five to sixty days), and a certain amount of time for the contractor to respond (typically twenty-one days), before a lawsuit can be filed. After receiving notice from the homeowner, the contractor can choose to inspect the house and offer to make the necessary repairs, offer to pay the cost of repairing the defect, or dispute the claim. In general, states requiring notice to cure also require that construction contracts outline the applicable notice-to-cure procedures.

---

quire a permit for roofing projects.) As discussed in chapter 2, the contractor, who should have experience working with your city or town bureaucracy, should be responsible for acquiring the proper permits and bringing building inspectors to your home to approve the new construction. Do not allow work to start until your contractor physically affixes evidence of a construction permit to your window. Even though the contractor is responsible for getting the permits, it is you who will have to deal with the expense and fines if the work is done without them.

The consequences of renovating without a permit can be disastrous. Your city needs to approve your renovation plans, and ensure that the plans meet the requirements of your local building code. If the city discovers that you have renovated without a permit, it may require you to tear down any completed work to confirm that the contractor's work is up to code—and, if it's not up to code, force you to bring it into compliance. The city will likely catch you when you sell your home, if it doesn't while the work is

TALKING TO A LAWYER

Q. We have a contract with a contractor for an addition to our home and a deck. The contract simply specifies a cost for each project, and a bottom-line total for all the work, without going into further detail about the project specifications. The contractor has just about finished the addition, and has been paid for his work up to this point, but we are un-happy with the work and want to stop the contract before he starts on the deck. If we stop now and end the contract, having already paid for the addition, does the contractor have any recourse against us?

A. A contractor will always have pretty strong grounds for a claim based on work that he or she has already performed. However, with respect to work that hasn't been performed yet, the tide may shift a bit. A good contract will spell out the exact specifications and scope of work that the contractor is to provide. Since that doesn't appear to have happened here, whether your termination of the contractor is justified will depend on the reasons for the termination. Was the contractor too slow? Was his work of poor quality? Did you just not like him? All of these questions must be answered. If a contract is vague or silent as to specifications or scope of work, courts and arbitrators will usually look to the custom in the industry with respect to performance issues. In other words, if the contractor failed to perform up to the standards of other contractors doing the same type of work in the same industry, the termination may be justified. Just bear in mind that a contractor can always sue you—regardless of how justifiable the termination may seem.

—**Answer by Darren Duzyk, Sullivan & Duzyk,
Lexington, Kentucky**

in progress. In many cities, before a home is sold, a municipal code inspector will inspect the home before granting a new certificate of occupancy. If the inspector spots illegal work, he or she will require you to prove that the renovations are up to code, a costly and time-consuming exercise that could also cause you to lose the sale. Don't be cheap and try to put one over on your city or county by not getting the appropriate permit for your project.

Attorney Fees and Arbitration

The contractor's standard contract probably will include language stating that he or she is entitled to attorney's fees and court costs in the event of litigation, with no reference to the homeowner's rights. In most states, these clauses are valid. In the event of litigation, such a clause would require you to pay all attorney costs and fees for yourself and the contractor, even if you are in the right and ultimately win the case. This type of clause obviously does not work in your favor, and you should try to negotiate a change. Instead, push for language stating that the prevailing party in any potential lawsuit is entitled to attorney's fees and court costs from the losing party.

The contract should also provide for arbitration in the event of a dispute. Arbitration is less formal than litigation in court, and is generally a faster and less expensive means of resolving disputes. A typical arbitration takes place in a law office, with an experienced attorney acting as **arbitrator** (judge). During the arbitration, the two sides argue their cases to the arbitrator, who makes a decision that is binding on the parties. Because an arbitration is a legal proceeding, make sure that your contract gives you the right to have a lawyer representing you. If the contract specifies that the arbitration will be conducted by a contractor industry group, rather than by an independent organization such as the American Arbitration Association, you could find the deck stacked against you in the event of a dispute. If you have any doubts, contact an attorney before you sign the contract.

THE WORLD AT YOUR FINGERTIPS

• Nearly all state contractor's licensing boards have websites. Visit your state board's site to see what must and should be included in a contract. The Permit Place website, at *www*

.permitplace.com/links/search1.asp, provides links to state, county, and city websites that contain information on permits and licensing.

• Chapter 7 contains more information on arbitration and other forms of dispute resolution.

REMEMBER THIS

• Take your time with the contract. The more specific the contract is, the better it is for both you and the contractor. Talking to a lawyer about the contract can save you time and trouble down the road.

• The contract needs to be in writing. An oral contract may be valid in your state, but proving the terms to which you and the contractor agreed orally can be very difficult.

• There is no such thing as a "standard contract." Feel free to negotiate with the contractor over clauses and costs. You have the most leverage at this point, before any money has changed hands.

• There are some issues that you must address in the contract, including mechanic's liens, warranties, cost, payment structure, start and completion dates, insurance, descriptions of the work, permits and inspections, and attorney's fees and arbitration.

CHAPTER 6

The Work

Ensuring Your Home Renovation Runs Smoothly

Richard and Susan hired a contractor to renovate their bathroom. They paid $7,500 for labor, and provided the materials themselves. After the contractor partially tiled the floor and tub surround, Richard and Susan inspected the job and observed several chipped corners, two very obvious cracks, and generally shabby workmanship. When they told the contractor about the cracks, he shrugged and said that nothing's ever perfect. A week later, the contractor built a partial wall, but it wasn't straight. Richard and Susan fired him on the spot. Now they are left with a gutted bathroom and work that has to be redone.

You've planned your renovation, selected a contractor based on estimates you've received, and signed a contract detailing the work to be performed, a payment schedule, and all the protections that you need to feel comfortable—at least from a legal standpoint. Now you hear a truck rumbling up your street with lumber to be dropped in your yard, the contractor is at your door holding rolled-up blueprints, and a platoon of happy subcontractors are whistling their way up the sidewalk. Your project is ready to begin.

Of course, the hard part is only beginning. Before your project can succeed, you must avoid a common construction pitfall: failure to start. Then, once work begins, you have to keep a close eye on its progress and communicate with the contractor to avoid delay and ensure that the work goes as you anticipate.

FAILURE TO START

One of the most serious—and frustrating—things a contractor can do is fail to start a job on time. A good contract prevents this problem by specifying an exact start date for the project. A contract that indicates only an approximate starting time—for example, a contract that obligates the contractor to start the project "within a reasonable time"—offers no such protection. After all, what constitutes a "reasonable time" is open to interpretation. In the case of poorly drafted contracts, a court may need to decide which side's interpretation is correct—and you don't want to wind up in court if you can avoid it.

A contractor may have reasonable excuses for failing to start your project on the agreed-upon date. Construction is always at the mercy of the weather; there can be delays in the supplying of materials to the contractor; and sometimes a contractor simply misjudges the date on which he or she will be available to start a project. However, even in situations where the contractor encounters reasonable delays, there is never an excuse for him or her not calling ahead to warn you of those delays.

Whether your contract indicates a specific starting date or you and the contractor simply have an oral agreement as to when the work will start, call the contractor immediately if your job doesn't start on the agreed-upon day. Better yet, it doesn't hurt to call a day or two before that date; this will let your contractor know that you're vigilant about the start date of your project. (If you don't want to appear pushy, say that you're simply confirming the workers' arrival time so you can make sure you're home to let them in.)

If the contractor doesn't start your project on time, he or she may have a good reason. But if not, then you should insist that the work start right away (if your contract specifies a starting date) or on a definite date in the future (if your contract is silent as to the starting date). If the work on your project starts late, responding immediately will let the contractor know that you're serious; this will help to establish a relationship of mutual respect. Most likely, the contractor will respond to your polite-yet-firm phone call with an apology and a revised starting date.

If the contractor doesn't respond in a satisfactory way, send him or her a registered letter (or a letter by certified mail, return

PUT IT IN WRITING

When you talk to the contractor about problems with your project—delayed starts or other issues—make notes of your conversation: the date and time you spoke, what you said, what the contractor said, and whether you resolved the problem or agreed to talk later. In case you run into serious problems and have to go to court, it's important for you to have a clear written or recorded statement of all your conversations with the contractor. Your memory of these conversations will probably be different from the contractor's—and if the project breaks down into a lawsuit, a claim based on careful notes will likely be more compelling to the court than your contractor's hazy recollections.

receipt requested) demanding a start date within a certain period of time—for example, within the next two weeks, or by a specific date in the future. Inform the contractor that a failure to respond as set forth in your letter will be considered a breach of your contract. Tell the contractor that if he or she fails to respond, you will demand a full refund of any deposit paid, and will hold him or her liable for any amount over his or her estimate that you have to pay another contractor.

If the contractor still fails to respond, then you should talk to an attorney. While we don't advocate running to a lawyer for every problem, a letter from your lawyer might be more effective in getting the contractor's attention. A short but firm letter should not cost a lot and may well be worth the cost. Keep in mind that busy contractors, like everyone else, will prioritize based on their perception of where the squeaky wheel is.

You can put additional pressure on the contractor by filing a complaint with the state licensing board, and by making a claim on the contractor's license bond. If the contractor has taken out a performance bond, you will want to contact the surety company as well.

If the contractor is a thief who never intended to do any work beyond talking you out of your deposit money, you have a big problem. Turn your case over to an attorney, the local prosecutor, and the state consumer protection division so justice can run its course. (Chapter 8 contains more information about fraud and misrepresentation.) Chances are, though, that this won't be necessary. If the contractor has failed to start your project, it's more likely that he or she simply mishandled scheduling and is hoping to avoid a confrontation with you. That's not an excuse or even a decent explanation, but if that's what's going on, a serious conversation should clear it up.

Big problems start with little problems. So if your project looks like it's going south on you right from the start, be prepared to unload your contractor; better to start all over again than to suffer through untold weeks or months pleading with the contractor to get on with the work. If you're spending your valuable time trying to force the contractor to do work he or she is not interested in performing, then the project is almost certain to fail.

DELAY

Like failure to start, another common complaint made by homeowners relates to delay after projects have begun. As noted earlier, construction is all a matter of timing; one day's delay in the arrival of supplies, or a plumber getting sick and needing two days' rest, can cause several days—or even weeks—of delays. As the homeowner, make sure you keep your end of the bargain: don't blame the contractor for delays that result from your own change of mind, and understand that there will sometimes be pauses or delays in the work, some of which will be out of the contractor's control. Having said that, the contractor has two major responsibilities: first, to keep the job moving along; and second, to keep you in the loop regarding any foreseeable problems or delays. The bottom line? Be understanding, because Murphy's Law often applies to construction scheduling, and each unforeseen delay may have an inordinately large impact on other aspects of the project. But also be firm in your expectation that everyone cooperate to the greatest extent possible to advance the project.

Your contract should protect you against unwarranted delays. If it does, bring the clause quickly to your contractor's attention in the event of a delay. If it doesn't, you still need to talk to the contractor to find out the cause of the delay and the date on which the job will restart. If the contractor has failed to warn you ahead of time about the delay, tell the contractor that a failure to communicate is unacceptable.

As with failures to start on time, delays are common and should be addressed quickly and calmly. If delays persist for an extended period of time—days turning into weeks turning into months—then take the steps discussed earlier in this chapter on

 TALKING TO A LAWYER

Q. *We hired a contractor to build a master-bedroom addition to our home. We signed a contract with no completion date, but the contractor told us the job would take three months. It is now nine months later. The room is framed and roofed, but other than that there's nothing in the room—only the subflooring. We have already paid the contractor half of the total price, and now can't get him to finish the work. What should we do?*

A. Send a demand letter (by registered or certified mail) reminding the contractor of his oral representation. Demand that he contact you by a specific date, that the work resume by a specific date, and that the work be completed within a reasonable, specific amount of time. Send copies of your letter to the appropriate licensing entities.

—Answer by R. Stephen Hansell, lawyer, patent attorney, and construction arbitrator, Florence, Montana

failure to start: write a registered or certified letter, contact an attorney, and cross your fingers.

FAILURE TO COMPLETE

The third leg in the contractor's dreaded "triangle" of delay and failure is failure to complete a project. But there's a huge difference between failure to start and failure to complete. "Failure to complete" generally translates to: "My house is completely torn up, no work has been done for months, and I can't get the contractor to return my calls."

Frankly—and we're not blaming the victim here—a homeowner should never let a project get so out of control that a simple project (say, a three-month renovation) is still only "near to completion" after twelve months. When a contractor behaves unprofessionally by essentially walking off the job, the problem should be addressed well before it reaches the disaster stage.

This is serious stuff, but it's the stuff that contracts are meant to address. As discussed in chapter 5, your contract should clearly indicate a completion date as well as a starting date, penalties to be applied in the event of contractor delays, and acceptable excuses for such delays. To reemphasize what was stated in the previous chapter, the contract is your opportunity to define acceptable boundaries for your contractor's behavior, and the penalties for not respecting those boundaries. If your contract fails to do so, the question of what constitutes "reasonable" behavior will arise yet again. And when it does, the ambiguity of the term "reasonable" will allow the contractor room to argue his or her case. Is it unreasonable for a three-month project to remain unfinished after six months? How about after nine months? A court will have to decide—and that means more time before your project is finished, or even restarted.

If you're working with a contractor who appears to have abandoned your project, you have to accept that you're not working with a responsible or competent professional. Don't waste your time wringing your hands and trying to figure out ways to get the contractor back on the job. If you can't get in touch with the contractor, or if he or she keeps putting you off, and the project is months behind schedule, assume that he or she has decided to abandon the job. See an attorney and get the ball rolling to force the contractor off the job and eliminate the possibility of mechanic's liens being filed against you or your property.

SHODDY WORKMANSHIP

Delays in starting and finishing a project are serious, but once the job is complete, the urgency you feel generally recedes to the level of irritation. Whether delays were so irritating that you'll never use that contractor again, or they simply become something to grouse about with friends while you're sitting in your renovated family room, if the job was done well, delays seem less important. But if the work wasn't done well, it's a very different story. Poor work will stay with you—and your home—for a long time.

A contractor's work must meet certain standards. Many of these standards are established by states and municipalities in their building codes, and relate primarily to structural safety: the thickness of beams, the maximum height of thresholds in doorways, the minimum number of required electrical outlets, the amount of outdoor air provided by mechanical ventilation, and so forth. There are also standards dictated by the trade and by customs of practice.

When inspecting your property in connection with a renovation, a city or local inspector will be looking for code violations. For example, if the weight on your floor will be increased by a new bathtub or kitchen appliance, the supporting structure will have to meet the gravity load requirements of the International Building Code. As another example, the fittings used in plumbing must meet thickness and materials requirements— for instance, the International Building Code prohibits "joints between different diameter pipes made with elasto-metric rolling O-rings." Fortunately, homeowners aren't responsible for code compliance—so you don't have to check to see whether the plumber is, in fact, using elasto-metric rolling O-rings, or whether the contractor has installed the required minimum amount of insulation in your walls. That's why the building inspector visits your home; ensuring compliance is his job.

You can, however, be alert for obvious signs of shoddy workmanship. You may need to look closely, but you don't need any professional knowledge to see that corners don't meet, that the faces of a cabinet aren't flush, or that a sink doesn't quite fit. If the contractor has slapped a lot of caulk on a window, it's a sign that the installation of that window is out of plumb. Basically, the construction should look clean and it should look square. If the work appears sloppy, then it probably is.

Keep in mind that the consequences of shoddy workmanship affect more than just your home's appearance. In addition to looking sloppy, a poorly constructed room can experience leaks, a poorly installed floor or ceiling can sag, and faulty electrical wiring can cause fires—to name just a few examples. It's not a stretch to say that shoddy workmanship can not only reduce the value of your home, but can also create dangerous situations for you and your family.

When you see signs of poor-quality workmanship, talk to the contractor immediately to resolve the problems as soon as possible. Take photographs or videos of the shoddy work, even if the contractor agrees to fix it. If he or she resists taking responsibility, then it's probably time to hire an independent inspector to evaluate the work. Your contract should provide you with the right to an independent inspection during the course of the project. Remember: One advantage of a well-drafted contract is that, in the event of resistance from a poorly behaved contractor, you can fall back on the terms of the contract to protect yourself.

The independent inspector can be a general expert in construction, or an expert in specific areas such as carpentry or electrical work. You can find experts through trade associations or informally through recommendations from people you already know; an expert can even be another contractor. Ideally, you'll

TALKING TO A LAWYER

Q. *I hired a contractor to repave my driveway and to fix some brickwork on my home that was falling apart. After the work was done, I paid him and thought everything was fine. But there's been some heavy rain in my area lately, and now the house is flooding, which wasn't happening before the work was done. I asked another contractor to examine the work, and his opinion is that the original contractor skimped on materials and did not do the job to code. What can I do?*

A. Contact the original contractor (by registered or certified mail) and demand that he repair the work by a specific time. Inform him that if he doesn't respond, you will have the work repaired yourself, and that he will be responsible for the added expense.

   If you do not receive a satisfactory response, you should contact a lawyer. You might be entitled to additional remedies or relief, and sometimes a letter or call from a lawyer carries more weight than contact from the homeowner.

   —**Answer by R. Stephen Hansell, lawyer, patent attorney, and construction arbitrator, Florence, Montana**

want the inspector to prepare a report indicating the problem, its cause, how it can be fixed, and the likely cost of the repairs.

If you present an inspector's report to your contractor and he or she still refuses to fix the problems, you need to start preparing for the possibility that you'll have to go to court. Talk to a lawyer right away, because he or she will want you to start preparing evidence: gathering notes of your conversations with the contractor, taking pictures of the defective work (if you haven't done so already), and taking whatever steps are necessary to ensure that you're in a good legal position. Being in a "good legal position"— or, as lawyers refer to it, "a good posture"—means not doing anything that can muddy your case. Don't tell the contractor that the problems are not a big deal, and don't try to fix them on your own.

WHAT CONSTITUTES SHODDY WORKMANSHIP?

Here are some signs of poor-quality workmanship:

Decks:

Improper drainage

Poor transition from the deck to the door or the threshold

Poor transition from the deck to the wall

Roofs:

Incomplete sheet-metal flashing

Poor installation of gutters

Improper slope to drain

Showers:

Joints not sealed with a coat of ceramic-tile mastic before tile installation

Gap between the base of the green board and the tub or shower pan is less than $1/4$ inch

Lack of flexible sealant joint at the tile-to-tub or shower pan juncture

Windows:

Inadequate waterproofing

Water leaks through product corners

Omission of butyl sealant bead around bottom and sides of window units

Noises:

Audible footsteps or voices from above, from below, or to the side

Audible tub and toilet draining from above

Faucets can be heard when turned on or off

Water hammer or humming noises

Pipes shaking

Be aware that you're in a legal situation and that, although it's not a criminal case, whatever you say or do can be used against you in court. A lawyer also can help you get your project back on track—if it's not already derailed.

HIDDEN PROBLEMS

No matter how well you plan your project, it's hard to know what lies beneath the surfaces of your home. Indeed, it is not at all unlikely that you will find big surprises when wallboard is stripped away or a floor is pulled up. In older homes, it is not uncommon to discover out-of-date electrical wiring and plumbing, or the presence of hazardous materials such as asbestos and toxic molds. Whatever problems you and your contractor discover, you'll have to deal with them before the project can proceed.

Deficiencies in wiring, plumbing, heating, and ventilation are likely to require at least minimal additional work by the contractor. In the case of wiring or plumbing that is not up to code, the simplest solution may be to remove it, particularly if you were planning to rewire or replumb that part of the house anyway. On the other hand, if you began your project with the assumption that your wiring or plumbing was up to code, then bringing the wiring or plumbing into compliance may constitute a significant expansion of your planned project. In that case, you and the contractor will have to write change orders to account for the additional work. (In your contract, don't forget to insist on written change orders; see chapter 5 for more information.)

Renovation projects may also be plagued by hidden environmental problems. Many older homes feature walls painted with lead paint, pipes wrapped in asbestos, asbestos used as insulation, or moisture that has built up over the years and fostered mold growth in damp areas. Asbestos was banned in 1977, and lead-based paint was banned in homes in 1978; thus, in houses built after the late 1970s, the primary environmental concern will be mold.

Asbestos

Asbestos is typically found in piping insulation, exterior shingles, and floor tiles. If it is undisturbed, it is not hazardous; asbestos only becomes dangerous when it flakes off into miniscule fibers and floats into the air where it can be inhaled.

Asbestos will be a concern during the demolition phase of your project. It is the contractor's responsibility to determine if asbestos will be disturbed during demolition. If the contractor finds asbestos, he or she is legally obliged to notify the homeowner and any workers who might come into contact with it.

If you learn that asbestos will be disturbed during your renovation, you need to get rid of it by hiring a contractor who specializes in asbestos removal. Asbestos is not a problem to approach casually; quite literally, it is deadly serious. Don't try to save money by removing it yourself or by paying your existing contractor to remove it if he or she is not specifically qualified to do so. Find an asbestos professional and get the job done right.

If you are unsure whether asbestos is present in a material in your home, you can bring a sample to a specialty laboratory for testing. (You can find specialty labs in the Yellow Pages under "Laboratories—Analytical.") Take care in handling the sample and be sure to keep it damp—remember, it's the flaking that releases the asbestos fibers.

If you think you have asbestos in your home, check the affected sites regularly for signs of damage. If the material believed to contain asbestos is in good condition, it will not release fibers, and often the best practice is to leave it alone. If the material is damaged, you can either have it repaired or have it removed.

Repair usually amounts to sealing or covering the asbestos material. Sealing involves application of a sealant, which binds the asbestos fibers together or coats the material to prevent release of the fibers. Pipe, furnace, and boiler insulation repairs are often handled by sealing. Don't do it yourself; hire an as-

LOOKING FOR ASBESTOS

Until the 1970s, many building products and insulation materials contained asbestos. Examples of such products and materials include:

- Steam pipes, boilers, and furnace ducts, which were often insulated with asbestos blankets or asbestos paper tape. If these insulation materials are damaged, or repaired or removed improperly, they can release asbestos fibers.

- Vinyl asbestos, asphalt, rubber floor tiles, the backing on vinyl sheet flooring, and adhesives used to install floor tile. Sanding or scraping these tiles can release fibers.

- Cement sheet, millboard, and paper used as insulation around furnaces and wood-burning stoves. Cutting, tearing, or sanding the insulation can release asbestos fibers.

- Soundproofing or decorative material sprayed on walls and ceilings. If these materials become loose, crumbly, or water-damaged, they can release fibers.

- Patching and joint compounds for walls and ceilings, and textured paints. Sanding or scraping these surfaces may release asbestos.

- Asbestos cement roofing, shingles, and siding. These products are not likely to release asbestos fibers unless they are cut.

bestos professional. Covering involves placing a protective wrap over asbestos-containing material to contain the asbestos fibers. Of course, this leaves the asbestos in place, but is much less expensive than removal.

If you need to remove asbestos-containing resilient floor coverings (linoleum or sheet vinyl and floor tiles), the best practice is to leave the flooring in place and install the new flooring over it. If the existing flooring has to be removed, have the removal done by an asbestos professional.

ASBESTOS DO'S AND DON'TS

- Do take every precaution to avoid damaging asbestos material.
- Don't dust, sweep, or vacuum debris that may contain asbestos.
- Don't saw, sand, scrape, or drill holes in asbestos materials.
- Don't use abrasives to strip wax from asbestos flooring.
- Don't sand asbestos flooring.
- Don't track through your home material that could contain asbestos. If you cannot avoid tracking such material through your home, clean the affected area with a wet mop.

Lead

If your home was built before 1978, you should assume that the paint used in your home contains lead. As with asbestos, the danger from lead-based paint lies in the flaking; lead paint in good condition is not a hazard. Breaking into walls, removing moldings, replacing windows, and scraping paint in preparation for a repainting job can all release paint chips and lead dust. Exposure to lead dust and chips is harmful to anyone, but is particularly harmful to children aged six and under.

Ingested regularly by young children, small amounts of lead dust can cause delayed development, learning problems, lowered IQ, and hyperactivity. Larger doses can cause high blood pressure, anemia, and kidney and reproductive disorders in both children and adults. Perhaps the most important bit of information about lead is that it accumulates in the body and its effects are irreversible.

If you are going to remove paint, and you're unsure about how to proceed, you may want to hire a lead-paint detection and removal firm. In any event, do not use a belt sander, propane torch, heat gun, dry scraper, or dry sandpaper to remove lead-

IF YOUR HOME HAS LEAD PAINT

Approximately 57 million homes contain at least some lead paint. Before 1950, paint contained as much as 50 percent lead.

If lead is detected in your home, the simplest way to control exposure is through frequent damp mopping to control dust—not through vacuuming, which can disperse the dust. Pick up loose paint chips with duct tape. Wash your child's hands and toys frequently to reduce exposure. It's also important not to sand or scrape leaded paint.

---

based paint. Using these tools can create large amounts of lead dust and fumes, which can remain in your home long after the work is done. And it would be a good idea to temporarily move your family (especially children and pregnant women) out of your home until the work is done and the area is properly cleaned. If moving isn't an option, then you should completely seal off the work area.

Mold

Mold is everywhere, at least potentially. If it can grow on the cheese in your refrigerator, it can grow anywhere conditions are (or were) damp. So when a contractor opens up a wall, especially in a room where there is a lot of moisture (such as a bathroom), it is not uncommon for him or her to find mold.

Mold is nothing to shrug off. Aside from the unsightliness of green or black mold, toxic molds, when released into the air, can cause health problems, especially for people with allergies or respiratory conditions such as asthma. The presence of mold can also indicate a leakage problem. The discovery of mold might sidetrack your renovation project for a while, because you may need to find the source of leakage and fix it.

Removing mold is fairly simple. A solution of four parts water and one part chlorine bleach can remove mold from tile, concrete, grout, and other surfaces that are not harmed by the harsh chlorine. Fabrics, carpet, painted walls, and wood can be cleaned using nontoxic oxygen bleach. If you find a large area of contamination (more than ten square feet), you should contact an environmental specialist. This might sound like overkill—at this point you're probably wondering how many different kinds of specialists there can possibly be!—but a large area of contamination indicates a serious problem that can't be bleached away. At the very least, you don't want your home to be a musty place to live. More importantly, you should consider the potential health hazards.

Toxic Molds

Toxic molds are molds that create airborne toxic spores called **mycotoxins**. When inhaled in sufficient quantities, mycotoxins can cause effects ranging from memory loss, allergies, and breathing difficulties to lung and neurological damage. The effects of toxic mold will depend on the type of mold involved, how much contact a person has, the length of exposure, and the exposed person's level of susceptibility. Young children, the elderly, asthmatics, and people with allergies are most vulnerable to mycotoxins. People with existing respiratory illnesses should be especially careful, because toxic-mold exposure can cause mold infections within their lungs.

Reaction to Mold Odors

Some people have very strong reactions to the smells given off by molds. Those who are especially susceptible to mold odors may contract headaches, nasal stuffiness, nausea, or even vomiting. In particular, asthmatics often exhibit symptoms when exposed to certain odors.

Radon

Radon is a colorless, odorless, radioactive gas that is produced by the decay of trace amounts of uranium and radium in soil. After uranium and radon decay to produce radon gas, the radon gas then decays further into radioactive particles called **radon daugh-ters**, which can attach themselves to solid particles in the air and be inhaled by humans. Radon has been linked to lung cancer.

The danger for homeowners is that radon, while pretty harm-less outdoors because of its scattered concentration, can become concentrated—and thus harmful—inside the home. Radon gas can seep in through cracks in concrete basement floors and walls, and through floor drains and sump pumps. The best solu-tion is to reduce the level of radon concentration by increasing the airflow through your home, particularly in the basement. If you think there may be radon in your home, you can expose the air in your house to a commercially available radon detector, and then send the sample to a laboratory for analysis.

The American Lung Association has plenty of additional infor-mation about radon available on its website at *www.lungusa.org*.

CONTRACTOR BANKRUPTCY

Of all the things that can go wrong with your renovation project, one of the most devastating can be the filing of bankruptcy by your contractor. In all the other situations discussed earlier in this chapter, you ultimately have some legal recourse when your contractor fails—difficult and expensive as it might be. In the case of a bankruptcy filing, however, a contractor enjoys the pro-tection of the bankruptcy court.

Without going into too much detail about the complicated field of bankruptcy law, it's sufficient to say that the purpose of bankruptcy is to relieve overwhelmed debtors of the obligation to pay their bills, and to give them a chance for a fresh start. Often a bankrupt party has property that he or she can sell in order to pay creditors. As a homeowner, however, you're proba-bly not owed money by the contractor—so you won't count as a "creditor" for purposes of bankruptcy law. Unfortunately, this means that if a contractor goes bankrupt, you'll probably lose any money you've paid to him or her, and will have to hire some-one else to finish the job.

The first thing to do when you receive notice of a bankruptcy from your contractor is to find a lawyer, preferably one who specializes in bankruptcy law. The lawyer can look at the contractor's filing papers and determine whether you have any legal recourse. There are different kinds of bankruptcies, and it's possible—though not likely—that the contractor could somehow be required to finish your project.

The biggest danger you face in the event of contractor bankruptcy—aside from the hole in your roof or your half-completed bathroom—is the possibility that a subcontractor or supplier who wasn't paid by the contractor will file a mechanic's lien against your house. This possibility alone is reason enough to require that your contractor submit lien waivers from subcontractors and suppliers before you make periodic payments on your project. Without lien waivers, you'll be extremely vulnerable: if your contractor files bankruptcy and the subcontractors and suppliers comply with the procedures for filing mechanic's liens in your state, more than likely you will have to pay them in full what they are owed by the contractor. Payments you made to the contractor—under the assumption that he or she would pass them along to the subcontractors and suppliers—are irrelevant if the subcontractors and suppliers ultimately weren't paid. So you could end up paying for work twice. It's very important to discuss these issues with your lawyer.

On the other hand, if you insisted on performance and payment bonds when you and your contractor signed a contract for your project, you can contact the insurance company that underwrote the bonds and arrange for the job to be finished and the subcontractors and suppliers to be paid. (Chapter 5 includes more information about bonds.)

MISCONDUCT BY THE CONTRACTOR OR EMPLOYEES

In legal terms, the key question when it comes to misconduct is whether the misconduct was intentional or negligent. If something bad happens because a couple of subcontractors aren't paying attention to their work, or because they're goofing off—for example, if someone is hurt, or if damage is done to your home or your neighbor's home—the subcontractors' conduct will likely be considered negligent, and any damages would be covered by the contractor's or subcontractor's liability insurance. If the injury or damage is at all serious, you should check with a lawyer to make sure you understand your rights.

However, if the misconduct was intentional, then insurance doesn't apply (insurance covers accidental and negligent acts only). Intentional misconduct can be almost anything: theft, violence or threat of violence, or intentional damaging of your property or your neighbor's property, to name just a few. In the case of intentional misconduct by an employee of your contractor, the contractor may be liable for the employee's actions under certain circumstances. On the other hand, if an independent subcontractor committed the misconduct when the contractor wasn't around, most likely the subcontractor alone would be liable for any damages.

Keep in mind that intentional misconduct may constitute more than just intentional **torts** (wrongful acts) to be handled through civil lawsuits; such misconduct may also be criminal. You certainly want to contact your attorney in the case of intentional misconduct, but it may be a good idea to contact the police as well. You don't want to overreact—a petty theft might best be handled by demanding return of the stolen item and firing the person responsible—but you shouldn't hesitate to involve the police if the damage was serious or if you feel threatened.

If your contractor was not involved in the misconduct, and if he or she fires the person responsible and agrees without debate to make good on any damage, you may wish to regard the misconduct simply as an aberration, and have the contractor continue with the project. But if the contractor was involved with the misconduct, defends the actions of the person responsible, or is anything other than apologetic and forthcoming, you should fire the contractor immediately.

No matter what the specifics of your situation, and whether

you feel the contractor was at fault or not, you should notify the state contractor's licensing board and any local permitting agencies in the event of any misconduct on your contractor's watch.

And don't forget: In the event of misconduct, if you owe the contractor payment for work completed before the incident, more than likely you will still have to pay—or face the prospect of a mechanic's lien. Certainly a subcontractor who was not involved in the misconduct, and who hasn't been paid for the work he or she has performed to that point, is entitled to be paid.

FRAUD/MISREPRESENTATION

Most states have some version of a Consumer Fraud Act. These acts apply to forms of misrepresentation that are dishonest business practices, but that may fall short of the out-and-out swindling that characterizes criminal fraud. In the areas of home renovation and repair, the statutes tend to focus on misrepresentation (lying) about contract price or financing terms, or about the quality of materials used—whether it's the use of lumber with a lower grade than what was promised, or the substitution of cheaper, lower-quality materials for better ones. Many statutes also feature provisions relating to contractors' misrepresentation of their capabilities. For example, if a contractor performs work without a proper building permit, this could be a violation of the applicable consumer fraud law. The statutory provisions are similar from state to state, but you'll need to check your state's consumer fraud laws for the particulars. The appendix to this book provides links to consumer fraud websites in many states.

The real power of consumer fraud law is that most states provide for a homeowner to recover **treble** (triple) damages in a consumer fraud lawsuit. Thus, if a court finds that your contractor cheated you out of $20,000 by using substandard materials, the court has the option of awarding you three times your actual damages. This means that you could be awarded $60,000 for a $20,000 misrepresentation.

WHAT'S CONSUMER FRAUD?

Consumer fraud laws vary greatly among the states, so check your state's law before you start dreaming about treble damages. Here are some contractor practices that may constitute consumer fraud under the law:

- Failure to enter into a written contract
- Entering into a contract that does not specify when the work is to start, when it is to be completed, or how long it will take
- Failure to complete the work within a contracted time period without proper reason or cause
- Performing work that requires licensing (electrical or plumbing) without holding the required licenses
- Performing work without a building permit
- Seeking payment before it is due under the terms of the contract, or seeking payment in full before the work is complete
- Starting work and then failing to return to complete the work
- Substituting lower-quality materials without authorization
- Attempting to charge additional money for work claimed to be outside of the scope of the contract, without having a written and signed change order

A few specific forms of home renovation fraud are especially sleazy. The most egregious examples include contractors knocking on your door to solicit your business, contractors invading an area after a natural disaster, and contractors preying on the elderly. Although the details of the scams will vary, the common goal of contractors in these cases is to separate homeowners from their money before doing any work. Remember: A reputable contractor will take time to plan your renovation with you, even if it's as relatively straightforward as a roofing job. If you're being pressured to make a quick decision, especially if the decision involves handing over money before work begins, you're probably being scammed, so put on the brakes. And if you've already fallen for a scam, then you've been the victim of a crime. Don't beat yourself up; instead, contact the police.

One of the biggest problems homeowners face in starting a renovation project is finding a contractor who will take the time to provide an estimate. But a careful estimate is worth the wait. Remember: Good contractors are busy, and the last thing they want to do is to rush into a job. And any reputable contractor will take time to line up materials and assemble a crew of subcontractors before giving you a starting date for your project. If you're hearing otherwise from a door-to-door contractor, then show that contractor the door. Chapter 8 on "Government Agencies and Legal Protections" contains more information about what to do if you have been a victim of fraud.

THE WORLD AT YOUR FINGERTIPS

- The Environmental Protection Agency has websites devoted to asbestos and lead. Through the asbestos site, at *www.epa.gov/iaq/asbestos.html*, you can find out whether your state has a training and certification program for asbestos removal contractors. You can also link to more information about where there may be asbestos in your home. Through the lead site, at *www.epa.gov/lead*, you can find certified lead-based paint professionals in most states. You can also order a free packet of information about lead from the National Lead Information Center through the site.

- For much, much more information on toxic molds, visit the Mold-Help website at *www.mold-help.org*.

- The Federal Trade Commission's website provides information about common consumer scams. Visit *www.ftc.gov/bcp/menu-home.htm* to access a list of publications, including several dealing with home renovation scams.

REMEMBER THIS

• The best way to avoid timing pitfalls—such as failure to start, delay, and failure to complete—is to have a good contract, and to communicate with your contractor to ensure that the project stays on track.

• Although you may not know much about construction, if you look at your contractor's work closely, you can usually spot shoddy workmanship. Bring up any concerns with the contractor immediately.

• If your house is more than thirty years old, it probably contains asbestos and lead-based paint.

• A performance bond is good protection against a contractor going bankrupt in the middle of your project.

• Remember that good contractors have more work than they can handle. So if you're being pressured by a contractor to sign a contract, you're not talking to a good contractor.

CHAPTER 7

Resolving Disputes

When Renovations Go Wrong

Ben and Irene hired a contractor to build an addition to their house. The contractor hired a subcontractor to do the carpentry work. The carpenter has completed more than half of the framing, but has not been paid by the general contractor, even though Ben and Irene have paid the general contractor in full for this phase of the project. Now the subcontractor refuses to finish the framing and is threatening to place a lien on the house unless Ben and Irene pay him what he is owed. During this time, the contractor has failed to show up and seems to have abandoned the job. When Ben and Irene talked to other carpenters about finishing the work, they said that the subcontractor's work was poor, and that the job should be restarted from scratch.

Sometimes there comes a point when things have gone so wrong that there's no getting a project back on track. That "tipping point" is different for every job, and you will have to weigh your options when deciding whether to walk away from your contractor and start afresh. As an example, if your project is 40 percent complete (and the contractor has been paid for the work completed), and you fire the contractor and hire another one, the remaining 60 percent of the job is probably going to cost more than if the original contractor had stayed on the job. A new contractor will have start-up costs and will be picking up the pieces of someone else's work and correcting any defective work. If the additional time and cost of hiring a new contractor are worth it to you, then you've reached the tipping point.

NEGOTIATING SOLUTIONS

The best strategy for you, the homeowner, is to anticipate problems. Talk your way through the job in detail with the contractor ahead of time and try to figure out where you have uncertainty. Stay on top of the project and ask all the questions that come to mind; if you're unhappy about something, tell the contractor right away. Chapter 5 provides more tips on how to create a good working relationship with your contractor.

If the project is running into problems, and you are getting more frustrated every day, you need to take the initiative. Sit down with the contractor and express your concerns: "Look, I don't like the way things are going. We need to figure this out. My concerns are [A, B, and C]. I want this to work, but I need for you to get your eye back on the ball." Do this before finished work has to be ripped out and restarted. The worst sound you can hear on a construction project is that of a jackhammer destroying defective or unacceptable work.

If you believe there's been a breach of the contract—for ex-

 A CALM CONVERSATION

In a difficult situation, it is helpful to prepare yourself before you sit down with the contractor. In this context, "preparation" means thinking carefully about everything that concerns you, and organizing your thoughts so that the contractor understands what you're upset about.

Present your concerns to the contractor in a calm, professional manner. This will give the contractor the opportunity to respond to your complaints one by one. And make your complaints specific. Not only will this prevent the conversation from becoming emotional, but it will also give the contractor specific issues to which he or she can respond.

Keep in mind that contractors have been through all of this before. They've been yelled at by meaner people than you, so venting your anger isn't going to get the problems solved. The contractor's response to your anger is likely to be more anger—or some kind of soft-shoe that distracts you from your concern. You want to solve the problem, not win an argument—so keep your demeanor calm and professional.

STATE LICENSING BOARDS

Some state licensing boards have the power to order a contractor to respond to a homeowner's complaints, and many boards offer to arrange for alternative dispute resolution. State licensing boards can also discipline contractors. Chapter 8 provides more information on resolving disputes through licensing boards.

ample, if there has been unreasonable delay, cost overrun, or shoddy workmanship—then you need to give the contractor a heads-up, either in a phone call or (even better) a face-to-face conversation. To protect yourself, make notes of your conversation, summarizing your concerns and any agreements reached, and send it to the contractor. Keep a copy for yourself. Then talk again in a week or so to make sure the problem has been resolved. The more that you and the contractor honestly try to resolve problems, the better your chances will be of having the renovation go well. In the end, if you and the contractor can't reach a resolution, then it may be time to involve a lawyer. Ask your lawyer to write a letter detailing your concerns, and asking the contractor to fix the problems or face the legal consequences. A letter from a lawyer isn't going to scare a contractor, but it will tell him or her that you're prepared to do whatever it takes to resolve the problem. That threat, in itself, can sometimes motivate contractors to become more responsive to homeowner concerns.

ALTERNATIVE DISPUTE RESOLUTION

If your negotiations and your lawyer's letter haven't produced results, check your contract to see if it requires or allows **alternative dispute resolution (ADR)**—which includes mediation or arbitration—in the event of a dispute. A contractual commitment to ADR means that you and the contractor have agreed to allow a mutually acceptable third party to resolve the dispute without going to court.

Certain standard contracts specifically require arbitration in the event of a dispute, which is more restrictive than a general provision for alternative dispute resolution. While arbitration is less expensive than a lawsuit, it still can be very costly; a lawyer can give you an estimate of the cost.

If your contract does not specifically provide for ADR, you can nonetheless propose ADR after a dispute arises. If ADR is not an option for resolving your dispute, your initial letter and the lawyer's letter will provide you with a basis for a lawsuit, possibly in small-claims court. But whatever your means of resolving the dispute, your goal is either specific performance of the contract (which means that the contractor is forced to perform the work as agreed) or damages (which means that the contractor pays any extra costs you incur by having someone else complete the project).

Very few home renovation disputes go to trial. Why? Because litigation is extremely expensive, it takes a long time (in major urban areas it can take two to five years for a case to get to trial), and it doesn't advance the goal of getting your renovation completed. In the last fifteen to twenty years, mediation and arbitration have become popular methods of resolving disputes in a fraction of the time and at a fraction of the cost required for litigation.

In both mediation and arbitration, the contractor and the homeowner sit down with a neutral third party and talk through the issues of the case. Mediation is informal and non-binding. Arbitration, though less formal than a trial, involves presentation of evidence and legal arguments leading to a formal, binding decision. Mediation and arbitration are not mutually exclusive; you may be able to mediate, then arbitrate, then litigate any unresolved issues or appeal an improper arbitration award. But once an agreement has been reached or an award has been determined, a court is unlikely to overturn it.

WHAT RECORDS SHOULD YOU KEEP?

Whether you're headed for mediation, arbitration, or trial, you need to have the entire project documented when you visit your lawyer. Bring copies of any plans for the project, your contract with the contractor, notes of conversations, change orders, records of payments, photographs, and everything else related to the project. You don't want the mediator, the arbitrator, or the judge to land in the middle of a "he said, she said" dispute; you want to be the one who is clear on all the details. Keep a file with all papers related to the home improvement job, including:

- The contract and any change orders
- Plans and specifications
- Bills and invoices
- Cancelled checks
- Letters, notes, and correspondence with the contractor
- Lien releases and paid receipts from subcontractors and material suppliers
- A record sheet on each subcontractor, listing the work performed and the length of time the subcontractor has worked on the job
- Warranties
- Samples of materials used in your project
- Photographs and videos of the work in progress

Mediation

The goal of mediation is to find common ground and a way to make the relationship between the contractor and homeowner work. In other words, unlike a trial—or even arbitration—mediation is an attempt to get the two sides to stop fighting, settle their differences, and get back to work. In litigation—and, to a certain extent, in arbitration—the process can be so adversarial that, when it's over, neither side will want to have any future dealings with the other. The mediation process, on the other hand, allows for the continuation of a working relationship. The operative concept is "win-win" negotiating.

If the homeowner and contractor agree to give mediation a try, they select a mediator, either together or through their lawyers. The American Arbitration Association, the National Arbitration Forum, and local bar associations can all provide the names of mediators in your area, or you can use referrals. If possible, you should look for a mediator with a successful record of mediating home renovation or construction disputes. A mediator who knows the industry can help to make the process more efficient, which will save you money in the long run.

Another point to consider is whether the mediator prefers to take an active role in the negotiation, offering his or her own evaluations of the case throughout the mediation, or has a lighter touch and works mainly to keep the discussions on track. The first type of mediator, known as an **evaluative mediator**, may suggest an appropriate settlement and even argue to the parties that they should accept it. If you and the contractor want someone to tell you what your case is worth, or to provide a reality check on the strengths and weaknesses of your respective positions, hire an evaluative mediator. On the other hand, if you don't think you would respond well to that kind of pressure, you may work well with the second kind of mediator, known as a **facilitative mediator**.

The premise of mediation is that it is completely voluntary, and either side can withdraw at any time for any reason. This point is very important. One key to a successful mediation is the commitment of both sides to work to find a resolution. If either the contractor or homeowner is merely going through the motions, the mediation will fail. Usually, the parties share the mediation fee and are responsible for their own attorney fees.

Once you arrange for a mediator, he or she will want preliminary information on the nature of the dispute and the amount of money at stake. In addition, if there is a need for experts to offer

ARCHITECT AS MEDIATOR

If an architect has been involved in your project, he or she can also play the role of neutral arbiter. An architect is "neutral" in the sense that he or she is generally retained by homeowners, but has a great deal of experience in building and renovation, and has worked with enough contractors to be able to understand the contractor's point of view.

If you and your contractor decide to consult the architect as a mediator, you should not assume that the architect will be your ally. If the architect is going to be an honest broker, he or she will be leaning on you as well as the contractor to reach a compromise. A possible disadvantage to using an architect is that the architect is part of the construction industry. That alone doesn't necessarily imply a bias, but it can mean that the architect understands the contractor's frustration better than the homeowner's.

If your dispute with the contractor is difficult to resolve, but in reality is relatively minor, an architect may be the best person to quickly bring the two of you together and get the project back on track. But if the dispute is complicated and potentially expensive, you are probably better served by going through a more formal dispute resolution process.

opinions, the mediator will ask for expert reports. You should also discuss the issue of whether lawyers should be involved in the mediation. If the issues that the homeowner and contractor are disputing are relatively straightforward, and little money is at stake, it may not be necessary to have lawyers present. If the dispute is more complex, then lawyers could help to defuse difficult emotional issues and make a more cogent presentation.

The mediation itself usually takes place in the mediator's office or a hotel suite. The typical mediation begins with a general session at which all parties are present. The mediator might announce the ground rules for the mediation session, and then each side makes a presentation—much like the opening statements in a trial, but far more informal. After the presentations, the mediator is likely to ask each side where they stand on the major issues of the case, and will focus the parties' attention to help resolve those issues. Each party's responses to the mediator's questions will reveal its priorities regarding resolution of the dispute. The goal is to include everyone in a group effort to solve the problem.

 ## FACTORS TO CONSIDER WHEN HIRING A MEDIATOR

If you decide to try mediation, consider these factors when hiring a mediator:

Experience. Check whether the mediator has been in practice for a long time and has handled home renovation cases. But also realize that a talented mediator can pick up the issues fairly quickly, and could do a better job than one who knows the industry but is not as skilled at mediating.

Education and training. Ask for the mediator's resume and review it before making a decision. A mediator is likely to have a fine education and to have taken a course in mediation, but check to see whether he or she has also received specialized training in construction or home renovation disputes, or has taken courses in construction law.

Possible bias. Talk to the mediator to see if you detect a biased perspective. Many mediators and arbitrators in construction disputes have gained their experience in the construction industry, and may be more understanding of the concerns of the contractor than those of the homeowner.

Fee. Most private mediators charge between $150 and $350 per hour, depending on the market. You can expect to pay close to the hourly rate charged by lawyers in your area. Most lawyer-mediators charge the same rate for mediation as they do for their general (unspecialized) legal services. This cost is split equally between the parties.

Next the mediator will meet with both sides separately, seeking more information on the facts of the dispute and on each side's negotiating positions. Then, depending on what happens in the individual meetings, the mediator will bring the two sides together to start the process of mutually solving the problem. Often this process involves moving back and forth between separate sessions and joint sessions. In most cases, a mediation will take no more than a few hours. In very complex, high-stakes cases, a mediation can last three or four days. In litigation and arbitration, **ex parte communications** (discussions between just one party and the judge or arbitrator) are strictly forbidden. But in mediation they are the norm, and are confidential unless the parties authorize the mediator to convey their communications to the other side.

The practical advantages of mediation are that it is non-adversarial; it reduces the costs of resolving the dispute, which are generally calculated on an hourly basis; and it allows for the possibility of the homeowner and contractor continuing to work together after the dispute is resolved. An additional advantage of mediation is that you can participate but you don't have to agree to a settlement. If you have to proceed to arbitration or litigation, the contractor will have revealed his or her issues in the mediation, which will help you and your lawyer evaluate your case and plan for the next proceeding.

Arbitration

Your contract probably includes a clause requiring disputes to go to arbitration. If you have tried mediation and it has failed, or if you decided against mediation and you and the contractor can't work out your disagreement, then either one of you can refer to the contract and insist on arbitration. If the contract includes an arbitration clause and the contractor refuses to go to arbitration, you can file a motion in court to order the contractor to engage in arbitration. If the court makes such an order, then you can put the litigation on hold pending the outcome of arbitration.

If your contract states that you and the contractor agree to submit to mandatory arbitration, then arbitration is not a voluntary process. It is an opportunity to resolve your differences short of a trial and all the litigation that precedes a trial. An arbitrator's decision has the finality of a court ruling. It can be appealed to a court, but the court is likely to uphold the decision unless the arbitrator has overstepped his or her authority. Even arbitrator awards based on bad legal judgment have historically been upheld by courts. Arbitrators are required to make detailed disclosures of potential conflicts of interest; their failure to do so is one of the few reasons that a court might overturn an arbitration award.

Arbitration is a simplified version of a trial; there is no formal discovery and the rules of evidence are greatly simplified.

 WHO ARE THE ARBITRATORS?

As is the case with selecting a mediator, the parties can choose an arbitrator, or a panel of arbitrators—usually three. Arbitrators are independent third parties who can be chosen informally or through a dispute resolution center, the most well known of which is the American Arbitration Association (another is the National Arbitration Forum).

When selecting an arbitrator, an important criterion to consider is expertise in the field. In home renovation or construction cases, arbitrators are typically selected from a list provided by a dispute resolution center, and typically consist of architects, engineers, construction and real estate professionals, and attorneys who have attended seminars designed to qualify them as arbitrators. Arbitrators usually have a contractor or engineering affiliation, which can be a matter of concern for a homeowner headed for arbitration. Once you receive a list of proposed arbitrators, you have the right to object to anyone on the list. When both sides have registered their objections, the administrator of the dispute resolution center appoints the panel based upon the remaining names.

Arbitration is more formal than mediation, and therefore more expensive; you'll be paying for your lawyer to prepare for a hearing in which evidence is presented and the parties and witnesses offer testimony. Because arbitration is a private matter, you and the contractor will pay the arbitrator's fee.

Your contract may require you to use the American Arbitration Association (AAA) or the National Arbitration Forum (NAF), both of which are nonprofit organizations. If the contract so requires, then you will need to file your demand for arbitration with the AAA or NAF, and send a copy of the demand to the contractor. The AAA or NAF will then act as the administrator of the arbitration. In this role, the AAA or NAF acts much as a courthouse bureaucracy would, assigning an arbitrator to your case (or a panel of three, depending on the amount of money at stake and the contract terms), setting hearing dates, and generally keeping the process moving. If the AAA or NAF is not named in the contract, you may choose the AAA, NAF, or one of several other dispute resolution centers.

The arbitration hearing itself resembles a trial, but follows the far-less-formal procedures drawn up by the AAA or other dispute resolution group administering the arbitration. Lawyers for both sides present opening and closing arguments, offer evidence, and question witnesses, much as in a normal trial. The formal rules of evidence do not apply. This means that testimony containing hearsay—for example, testimony by a person who did not see something personally, but who wants to testify based on what someone else told them—may be allowed. Other kinds of evidence that could not be used in a trial may also be admitted. But even though it's not a trial, an arbitration still demands many of the skills required of trial attorneys: cross-examination, analysis of the issues, and the ability to make an organized, persuasive presentation of the claim. In contrast to a regular trial, the typical arbitration hearing lasts from a few hours to a few days for the most complex cases.

When the arbitrator makes his or her ruling, that ruling is called an **award** and has the finality of a court ruling. However, within the constraints of the law, the arbitrator has the ability to

ADVANTAGES AND DISADVANTAGES OF ARBITRATION

Advantages of arbitration include:

- *Efficiency.* Arbitration usually can be resolved sooner than court proceedings. The arbitration hearing should be shorter in length, and the preparation work less demanding.

- *Convenience.* Hearings are arranged at times and places that suit the parties, arbitrators, and witnesses.

- *Flexibility.* Arbitration procedures can be streamlined or simplified according to the circumstances and the parties' agreement.

Disadvantages include:

- *Cost.* One or both parties must pay for the arbitrator's services. For a claim up to $100,000, the minimum fee for a single arbitrator is $2,000; the maximum fee can reach 10 percent of the claim. In addition, the lawyers for each side will have to be compensated for preparation time and for time spent at the hearing.

craft a solution that grants partial relief to both sides—which can either make everyone equally happy or equally unhappy.

Small-Claims Court

Pursuing your contractor in a small-claims court may be another alternative for resolving your dispute. Small-claims court is a special type of court where lawyers are not allowed. Small-claims proceedings are fast, inexpensive, and informal.

To start a small-claims case, you go to the courthouse, fill out a small-claims complaint form, have it served on your opponent, and go to court at the appointed date and time. Depending on how crowded the court is, you'll probably get to court within a couple of months. In small-claims cases, you and your opponent represent yourselves. You stand in front of the judge, explain your complaint, and offer as evidence the paperwork and testimony that supports your claim; then your opponent does the same. Most of the time, the judge will hand down a decision within a day or two. Sometimes judges decide the case on the spot. Many small-claims courts are not courts of record, which means that they do not make written transcripts of their proceedings. This means that, when a small-claims judge makes a ruling, the judgment does not automatically attach (create a lien).

As the term "small claims" suggests, cases in small-claims court are limited to small amounts. In California and North Carolina, the limit is $5,000; in Arizona, it's $2,500. If the amount in dispute is more than the small-claims limit for your state, then by suing in small-claims court you will give up your claim to any amount over that limit. For instance, if you're a homeowner in California who believes a contractor owes you $7,000 and you decide to go to small-claims court, you may only claim and recover up to $5,000. You can't come back later and demand the other $2,000—one bite is all you get.

The advantages of going to small-claims court are speed and cost: your case will be resolved within months rather than years, and it won't cost you much more than the amount of the court filing fee and the cost of having the legal documents properly delivered to your opponent. However, small-claims litigation may be unsuitable if your claim is for an amount that exceeds the jurisdictional limit. If this is the case, you'll need to decide whether it's more important for you to have an amount equal to the jurisdictional limit ($5,000 in the above example) within a couple of months—assuming you win, of course—than it is to have the entire amount you are owed ($7,000 in the above example), minus attorney fees and court costs, a year or two down the road.

LAWSUITS

If all else fails, you can sue the contractor.

Lawyers file lawsuits all the time—hundreds of thousands every year. And for just that reason—because they are involved in lawsuits day in and day out—most lawyers will tell you that if you can settle your differences without filing suit, that's what you should do. A lawsuit will drain you—of your money, your time, and your energy—so if you're going to file one, it had better be worth it.

First, consider the expense of a lawsuit, and measure that cost against what you hope to gain when the litigation is over. A lawyer will help you to clarify not only what you want to gain, but, more important, what you are likely to gain. If the lawsuit is over a breach of contract—for shoddy workmanship or failure to complete, for instance—then it is very unlikely that you will be able to recover your attorney's fees and costs (court filing fees, process server's fees, court reporter fees for depositions, and so on), unless your contract provides that the prevailing party may be awarded fees and costs. For instance, if you are suing the contractor for $20,000, it's within the realm of possibility that your attorney's fees for going to trial could be around $10,000; and it's also possible that you could lose the suit entirely, or be awarded less than the $20,000 you think you are owed. So in reality, you could be filing a lawsuit that gives you an opportunity to get back $10,000 at the most, and maybe to get back nothing. On top of that, you won't get anything until three or four years down the road. Now these are made-up figures, of course. But you do need to sit down with your lawyer and do the math.

Second, think of the time it could take. In nearly every state, there are two levels of trial courts: **courts of limited jurisdiction** (often called "municipal courts," but the name varies among the states) and **courts of general jurisdiction** (which can be called "superior courts," "circuit courts," or "district courts," depending on the state). For civil cases, the major distinction between the two types of courts is that courts of limited jurisdiction can only hear cases involving claims for less than a certain amount (in California, the amount is $25,000; in North Carolina, it's $10,000; in Wyoming, it's $7,000). If your claim is for an amount below the jurisdictional limit, your chances of getting to trial in a lower court within a year are pretty good. But if the lawsuit is for an amount that exceeds the jurisdictional limit, then a trial will be anywhere from eighteen months to six or seven years away. The larger the population center, the more crowded its courts are. A lawyer who does litigation work can give you a fair estimate of the time involved.

Who Should You Sue?

The working assumption so far has been that any legal action by a homeowner would be against a contractor or subcontractors. But in fact, anyone who has been involved in the project is a possible defendant. The first step for the homeowner is to decide who should be included in the lawsuit. In most cases, the homeowner's lawyer will want to name everyone who had a hand in the renovation as a defendant in the case. Normally when a lawsuit is filed, it is not necessarily clear whether only the contractor is at fault, or whether the materials suppliers or the architect may also be at fault—so anyone who might have been at fault will be named as a defendant. This approach can cause some innocent people anguish, trouble, and money. But there's a good reason for it. If the homeowner's lawyer knows, for instance, that an architect drew up the plans for the renovation, and the lawyer does not name that architect as a defendant, court rules may prohibit the lawyer from later bringing the architect into the suit. The lawyer's failure to name a possible defendant could constitute attorney malpractice, which is another can of worms.

There is another reason to name every possible defendant, and that reason has to do with what's known as "deep pockets." When it comes to paying for any damages awarded in a lawsuit, the **plaintiff** (here, the homeowner) is looking for insurance policies and defendants with assets. You should have made certain when you signed your contract that the contractor had general liability insurance to cover any damage for which he or she will be responsible. Architects have professional liability insurance to cover hundreds of thousands of dollars worth of damage, and that's often enough incentive to include the architect in a suit. If the damages might be related to the materials used in the renovation, the suppliers will find themselves in the lawsuit also.

The Contractor

The contractor can be held liable on a number of bases, depending on the type of damage that has been done. If the damage involves a breach of the contract, the contractor can be held responsible for all the costs related to the breach. For instance, if the contractor walks off the job, the homeowner can potentially be awarded any payments made to the contractor for work the contractor didn't complete, the difference between the original cost of the renovation and the amount charged by the new contractor, any damage to the house itself that can be linked to the walk-off (such as weather damage to parts of the house left exposed), and any other physical or monetary damage suffered because of the breach. However, in contract breaches, the homeowner will not be entitled to damages for emotional distress, and it is unlikely the homeowner will be awarded attorney's fees and costs, unless provided for by the contract or by statute.

One additional note: because of a growing concern about abuses in the home renovation and repair industry, consumer fraud laws in a number of states now regulate some actions by contractors that would typically be considered simple breaches of contract. The treble damages provision in many consumer fraud laws can act as a big incentive for contractors to behave appropriately. For this reason, the threat of a lawsuit or of being reported to the state's consumer protection agency often carries a great deal of weight with contractors. Chapter 8 includes more information about federal and state laws in this area.

If the damage results from negligence on the part of the contractor or one of the subcontractors (in cases of shoddy workmanship, for example), the homeowner can recover the costs of actual damages to his or her home and all the reasonable costs associated with the damage, such as costs of repair. If the negligence results in a personal injury—say, if a pipe falls on the homeowner's head—then the homeowner could be awarded all of his or her medical costs and economic costs (costs from loss of income), along with damages for the pain and suffering involved in the injury. Personal-injury negligence cases are generally taken by lawyers on a contingent-fee basis, which means that instead of paying the lawyer by the hour, as is normal in a breach-of-contract case, the lawyer takes a percentage of the award as his or her fee. Depending on the difficulty of the case, and whether the case is settled before trial, contingent fees can range from 25 percent to 50 percent of the award, and are most often between 33 percent and 40 percent of the award. Some lawyers working on a contingent-fee basis will pay all the litigation costs even if you lose—if you win, the costs will come out of the award—but some will expect the client to pay the costs in a losing case. Before you sign a contingent-fee contract, make sure you understand the arrangement regarding costs.

If the damage is a result of intentional misconduct by the contractor, then not only can the contractor be held responsible for all the damages resulting from his or her negligence, but the court can also award **punitive damages**, which are damages awarded solely to punish the defendant for his or her conduct. If the intentional conduct is particularly egregious, the amount of punitive damages awarded could be staggering.

And if the contractor has defrauded you or intentionally misrepresented an important fact—such as the cost of the project, or the scope of a building permit so that part of your renovation work was illegal—that conduct could be covered by your state's consumer fraud law. As was mentioned above, the importance of consumer fraud statutes is that many of them call for treble damages against the defendant, as well as an award of attorney's fees to the plaintiff. If the contractor or a supplier made specific warranties or guarantees that were not honored, breach-of-warranty actions may provide additional relief.

The Architect

There are two ways for an architect to be liable: for negligence in drawing up the plans for a renovation; and for failure to properly supervise the project, when the architect has assumed supervision of the project as part of his or her role.

An architect's mistake in the planning stage can lead to complete disaster—where, say, the architect miscalculates the load-bearing capacity of a support structure and part of the house falls down. It can also create additional work for the contractor—work for which the homeowner will be charged. The realistic concern for the homeowner is that the contractor will not catch the architect's negligence in time, and that the homeowner will wind up with a finished product that is unsafe or off-kilter. The homeowner is then stuck deciding whether the mistake is so great that the entire job needs to be redone, or whether he or she should simply accept the inadequate job and try to assess the financial impact of a seriously imperfect room on the value of the home.

An architect can also be liable for failure to properly supervise a project. Some architects simply draw up plans and have no further involvement with a project once those plans are finalized; others take responsibility for keeping an eye on the job. In a residential renovation, the architect typically will not show up every day, but will monitor the project once a week or so to make sure the contractor is using the agreed-upon materials, following the plans, and doing an acceptable job. In addition, the contract may call for periodic inspections before work is covered up by drywall or other finish work. If the project runs into serious trouble, the architect may find himself or herself liable for breach of contract for failing to catch the contractor's mistakes.

The Materials Supplier

The supplier can be liable for delivering the wrong materials, either intentionally or negligently. If you provide in your contract for materials of a certain brand name and quality, you are entitled to have those materials used in the project. If the supplier delivers less-expensive generic materials instead of the brand-name materials you ordered, then you have been cheated—even if physical damage doesn't result because of the change. In that case, the supplier and the contractor may be liable under consumer fraud laws, and may be required to pay you an amount equal to the difference in value between the two types of materials. And if the use of lower-grade materials results in damage—for example, if low-grade roofing materials lead to leaks or a shorter service life—then the supplier, as well as the contractor, can be held liable for all the damage and repair costs.

Suing the Homeowner

Yes, it's true: The renovating homeowner can also be sued. The most basic legal danger for homeowners arises from the failure to make timely payments to the contractor, and from failure to ensure that suppliers and subcontractors have been paid by the contractor. Also, a homeowner who knows of a dangerous condition, such as a rotten floor or exposed wiring, and does not warn the workers, may be found liable for negligent or even intentional infliction of injury.

Mechanic's or Construction Liens

As has been noted in chapter 6, the only leverage the people who do renovation work have over a homeowner is the **mechanic's lien**, also known as a **construction lien**. If workers don't get paid, no matter what the reason, a lien may be placed on the homeowner's property. Even if the lien isn't enforced, it will sit there—a cloud on the title to your property—until you pay it off, it expires, or you get a court order to have it released.

When dealing with a slow or incompetent contractor, keep in mind that if you kick the contractor off the job, terminate the contract, or refuse to make any further payments, mechanic's liens could be lurking just around the corner. Before moving any further, understand that your primary defense against a mechanic's lien is to make sure that everyone has been paid for the work they have done and that you have received lien waivers from everyone you and the contractor have paid. Don't forget that you can also protect yourself from a mechanic's lien by requiring a payment bond from the contractor at the contract stage of the project. Payment bonds guarantee that everyone will get paid. Unfortunately, nothing can actually stop the filing of a mechanic's lien, even if it's unenforceable, but a payment bond makes filing such a lien unnecessary for an unpaid worker.

Mechanic's liens are **statutory** in nature, which means that: (1) every state's procedure for filing and enforcing a lien will be different; and (2) those procedures must be followed to the letter in order for the lien to be valid against your property. Two assumptions underlie the law here: first, that workers are entitled to get paid for their work, period; and second, because a lien on property is such a serious legal weapon, if a worker decides to use it, he or she must follow the law precisely or the courts won't support its use.

As different as various states' procedural requirements may be, the basic requirements for a mechanic's lien in any state involve notice to the homeowner. (Please note that the timing requirements discussed here may not apply to your state; laws vary, so check your own state's law for the applicable requirements.) Within a certain number of days after starting the work, the contractor or subcontractor is required to file a **preliminary notice** alerting the homeowner to the worker's right to place a lien on the property. Generally, the preliminary notice must be filed from between twenty and ninety days after works starts. To make sure that the homeowner actually receives the preliminary notice, most statutes require that the notice be sent to the homeowner by certified or registered mail, or delivered in person. In many states, subcontractors and material suppliers do not have lien rights if they do not file a timely notice, which means that sometimes a lien notice may be filed simply to meet time constraints, even if payment is ultimately made. The bottom line is that receiving a preliminary notice does not necessarily mean that a lien is going to be filed against you—it just means that the worker or supplier is safeguarding his or her future right to demand payment if something goes wrong.

The lien itself must be filed with the county where the home is located. The lien must be filed within the time constraints of the state statute; if not, it is unenforceable (see below). After the lien has been filed, **notice of the lien filing** has to be sent to the homeowner by certified or registered mail, or personally served. If this notice is untimely, the homeowner can demand that the lien be removed.

The last stage of the lien process is **enforcement**. The contractor or subcontractor must file a lawsuit to enforce a valid lien—that is, to have a court order the sale of your home to pay off the lien—within a certain time period, which can be from ninety days to two years after the date the lien is recorded. If no suit for enforcement is filed within this time period, then the lien expires and is no longer enforceable. But that doesn't mean you don't have anything to worry about. Even if the lien is no longer enforceable, it will still appear on a title search and will stay attached to your property until you act to remove it.

To remove a valid lien, you can pay the amount claimed on the lien, or negotiate a lower payment with the contractor or subcontractor. You can also fight the lien in court.

If you think the lien is invalid, you should write a demand letter requesting that the invalid lien be removed. Such a letter is sometimes enough to convince the lienholder to remove the

 TALKING TO A LAWYER

Q. I hired a contractor to remodel my kitchen. The job is complete, except for some touch-up work. But now the subcontractor who supplied and installed the countertops says that, because of a dispute with the general contractor over a different job, the general contractor has not paid him for the work on my kitchen. The subcontractor said that he is owed $3,000 and will place a lien on my home if I don't pay him immediately. The contractor then called me and said not to pay anyone until he and the subcontractor resolve their dispute. I still owe the general contractor $5,000. Is it time for me to hire an attorney?

A. Not quite yet. As you have been notified of the dispute, continue to withhold the funds from the general contractor until you receive a release saying that all the subcontractors have been paid in full. For extra protection, ask to receive a specific release, including a release of lien rights from the subcontractor in question.

—**Answer by Michelle Gerred, NCS,**
Highland Heights, Ohio

INJURY ON THE JOB

You and the contractor ought to have insurance to cover on-the-job injuries. The contractor needs to have workers' compensation insurance to cover injuries to employees and subcontractors. If the subcontractors are independent contractors, make sure that they have workers' comp coverage. In many states, they will be covered by the contractor's coverage; in some states they will need their own. As discussed in chapter 4, workers' compensation provides a form of insurance to workers; if they are injured on the job, it will pay their medical and additional expenses. Workers' comp also means that the injured worker is not entitled to sue the employer over the negligence that may have caused the injury.

The contractor also needs to have general liability coverage for injuries to anyone not working for him or her; and you need to make sure that your homeowner's policy covers any possible injury that could occur during your renovation. Before the renovation starts, talk with your insurance agent and upgrade your policy or add a general liability policy if necessary.

lien. You can also file a **notice to commence suit** in court to remove an invalid lien. This notice requires the lienholder to file a lawsuit or release the lien. This action should not be taken lightly: if the lienholder feels that he or she has a valid lien, the lienholder could and will file the lawsuit to foreclose the lien.

Your title insurance company might also help in having an improper lien removed.

How Does a Lawsuit Work?

From the beginning to the end of a lawsuit, the litigation process generally grinds along very slowly.

The first step in a lawsuit is the complaint, which is a statement of the basic case: the defendant's breach or negligence, the damage to you, the legal theories that support your case, and the demand for relief. The complaint is personally served on each defendant, who then has twenty to thirty days to file a response. The response generally denies that the events detailed in the complaint actually happened, or denies responsibility for those events, or denies the amount of the damages.

Then the lawsuit enters the **discovery** phase, where both sides try to find out everything about the other side's case by examining the contract, notes of conversations between the parties, receipts for payments, and so on. At this point, lawyers for each side take **depositions** (testimony given under oath, usually in a lawyer's office), and exchange interrogatories and other formal requests for information.

Finally, after several years, the case will go to trial. At trial, you put forward all your evidence to a judge or jury, who decides whether you win or lose—and, if you win, how much the defendant has to pay you. But even after the trial, the process may not

---

 ## STATUTES OF LIMITATION

Statutes of limitation are the laws that dictate how long you have to file a lawsuit after suffering damages, injury, or loss. All states are different, of course, but the limitation period can be anywhere from a year to three years, five years, or even ten, depending on the state and on the type of legal problem. If you try to file a lawsuit after the applicable statute of limitation expires, the suit will be invalid and you might be held responsible for filing a frivolous lawsuit—even if the actual claim is legitimate. Generally, personal-injury suits must be filed within one to two years of the injury; breach of contract suits may have a limitation period of three years or longer.

Whatever the limitation period in your state, you have the responsibility to see a lawyer as soon as possible after you realize you have suffered damage. It may be that the damage to your house from shoddy workmanship will not show up for months or even years, but as soon as you know (or should know) that you have suffered damage, you have to begin the legal process in order to protect your right to sue.

be over; if a great deal of money is at stake, it's very likely that the losing side will appeal, which can add a year or two to the process. The defendant may be bankrupt or **judgment-proof** (have no money and no assets from which the judgment can be satisfied) by then.

During all this time, which is filled with motions before the court and occasional hearings, the lawyers are probably working to settle the case. Only about 5 percent of all lawsuits ever reach trial, so a great deal of the work the lawyers are doing in the years before trial involves trying to get a clear picture of the case, so both sides can agree on what happened and settle on the damages. Settlement can be a bitter pill to swallow, because it means having to give something up (usually money you thought you were owed or would win at trial) in order to achieve certainty and closure. But every lawyer knows a trial is a gamble, and a good lawyer knows a good settlement when he or she sees it.

THE WORLD AT YOUR FINGERTIPS

- You can find more information about mediation, and locate a mediator in your area, at the Mediate.com website at *www .mediate.com*.
- You can read more about arbitration, and find an arbitrator for your dispute, at the websites of the two biggest nonprofit arbitration centers. The website of the American Arbitration Association is at *www.adr.org*; the website of the National Arbitration Forum is at *www.arb-forum.com*.
- For a sample pamphlet of information on small-claims courts, visit this site devoted to the Virginia court system: *www .courts.state.va.us/pamphlets/small_claims.html*. While the information is specific to Virginia, the pamphlet is comprehensive, and Virginia's procedures are similar to small-claims procedures in other states.
- For information on the court system in your state, visit the website of the National Center for State Courts, which features

links to court websites in every state: *www.ncsconline.org/D_KIS/ info_court_web_sites.html#State*.

REMEMBER THIS

- If you have a dispute, the best course of action is to avoid litigation, if possible, by resolving it informally with the contractor. However, you should be prepared to file suit if you can't resolve the dispute through other means.
- If you can't solve your problems informally, it's a good idea to try mediation. Mediation only works if both sides agree to it and are committed to the process, but it allows for the possibility that you and the contractor can continue working together.
- Your contract probably includes a clause requiring disputes to go to arbitration. It is a more formal process than mediation and will take more time, but it should avoid the time and expense of litigation.
- If the amount of money in dispute is relatively small, consider small-claims court, even if you would have to give up part of your claim in order to fall within the small-claims jurisdictional limit. It could save you thousands of dollars in attorney's fees and court costs.
- If you have exhausted all other options and you decide to sue someone, or if someone sues you, you will definitely need a lawyer. Chapter 9 provides more information about working with a lawyer.

CHAPTER 8

Government Agencies
and Legal Protections

Some Protection
from Unscrupulous Contractors

Jim and Teresa had problems with their contractor almost from the day they signed the contract to have their kitchen and first-floor bathroom renovated. The contractor demanded a $10,000 deposit, dropped the lumber into their backyard a week after the contracted start date, and then didn't show up again for two weeks. The work, Jim and Teresa think, is slipshod. Moreover, the contractor keeps demanding payments before the periodic dates scheduled in the contract, and has generally been difficult to work with. Teresa checked with the state licensing board, which confirmed that the contractor was licensed, but wouldn't give her any more information. Jim and Teresa don't want the expense and trouble of a lawsuit, but they think there must be some government agency out there that could help them bring the contractor into line.

In the area of home renovation, there's no excuse for uttering the age-old complaint, "there oughta be a law." Why? Because plenty of federal and state laws and agencies exist to protect homeowners from incompetent and unscrupulous contractors. Most states have contractor licensing boards (listed in the appendix to this book) to discipline incompetent and dishonest contractors. Nearly all states have consumer fraud laws that regulate contractors' actions. And several states have homeowner recovery funds to compensate homeowners for losses caused by contractors. Federal laws such as the Consumer Protection Act, the Magnuson-Moss Warranty Act, and the Truth in Lending Act can also help protect homeowners.

Nonetheless, as a homeowner, your best protection against disaster is your own good sense, some good luck, and a surety bond. This is not to say that government agencies don't do good work, but from the homeowner's standpoint, the government too often gets to the party too late with too little. It's not as if these agencies are blind to the problems contractors have created for homeowners, but their real focus is to stop dishonest contractors from hurting more people. Most government agencies are basically enforcement agencies whose job is to keep the bad contractors out of the contracting business. They do not provide substitutes for civil lawsuits. A lawsuit usually remains the homeowner's only real weapon for recovering losses. (Chapter 7 provides more information about forms of alternative dispute resolution and lawsuits.)

With those words of warning in mind, this chapter outlines the local, state, and federal laws and agencies that may be able to protect you from bad contractors, and help you if something has gone wrong.

LICENSING BOARDS

Most states have an agency or division that licenses contractors. It might go by the name "State Contractors Licensing Board," "Registrar of Contractors," "Construction Industry Licensing Board," "Department of Labor and Industries," or any number of other titles. But whatever their names, all licensing agencies license and discipline contractors. Most of the time, they also supervise a fund to compensate homeowners for damages and losses caused by contractors. Licensing agencies have the ability to revoke a contractor's license. In states that consider contractor misconduct to be a criminal matter, licensing boards can also refer a matter to the state attorney general's consumer protection division.

Licensing boards generally maintain information about the status of contractors. They will be able to tell you whether contractors are currently licensed and whether there are any construction-related civil judgments against them. They can also tell you whether a contractor has paid a licensing bond, and the amount of any bonds he or she carries. In Massachusetts, the Office of Consumer Affairs will also tell you whether the contractor has lost any arbitration cases or has had any guaranty fund claims filed against his or her registration. In some states, privacy laws may restrict information about complaints filed against contractors, particularly those that have not been resolved.

Though many states maintain information about contractors, many other states license only specialty contractors—such as electricians and heating and air-conditioning contractors—or do not license contractors at all. In those states, licensing and enforcement falls to local governments, either county or municipal.

Licensing agencies also take complaints about contractors. Whether you're dealing with a state or local licensing agency, the process remains substantially the same: you file a complaint, and the agency investigates. The agency may then try to settle the case informally, or order the contractor to fix the problem or compensate the homeowner. If that doesn't work, the agency holds an administrative hearing and then decides what discipline against the contractor, if any, is warranted. While it varies from state to state, such discipline can include anything from a fine to suspension or revocation of the contractor's license. Unfortunately, because they are government bureaucracies, the agencies have to operate in strict accordance with procedures that allow both sides time to make their arguments. This means that, in the words of one licensing agency representative, obtaining assistance "is not a swift process." But however slow the process may be, having a complaint filed with a licensing agency is not good for a contractor's business, and the threat of filing such a complaint can be a valuable bargaining tool for the homeowner in a dispute with a contractor.

State licensing boards are probably a homeowner's best bet for governmental action that can have a direct impact on a contractor. But licensing boards can't suspend or revoke a contractor's license without evidence of incompetence or dishonest conduct. Unfortunately, such evidence often consists of the ruins of your new family room, or of payments you made for work never performed.

As a side note, licensing agencies generally don't deal with unlicensed contractors; in most states, unlicensed contracting is a crime, so the unlicensed contractor is more likely to have dealings with the police than with a licensing board. This is yet another good reason to avoid an unlicensed contractor: licensing boards generally cannot help you in a dispute with a contractor who is not licensed, though some states may allow a homeowner to avoid payment in such cases.

Make sure you know what protections, if any, your state provides. And remember: if your state government doesn't regulate contractors, more than likely your county or municipal government does. The appendix to this book lists state licensing boards. More information about this topic is generally available on state government websites, often under the heading "consumer protection" or "professional regulation"; if you can't find the necessary information under these headings, visit your state attorney general's Web page or phone his or her office.

COMPLAINT PROCEDURES IN ARIZONA

In Arizona, the Registrar of Contractors handles complaints about licensed contractors.

When a complaint has been filed against a licensed contractor, a copy of the complaint is mailed to the contractor, and the complaint is assigned to a construction inspector who decides if there are workmanship questions that require a job site inspection.

The inspector will evaluate information gathered through inspections, plans and specifications, building codes, analysis of workmanship standards, and data supplied by the contractor and the homeowner. He or she will then decide whether the complaints are valid. If the inspector concludes that the allegations have no merit, the inspector will notify the contractor and homeowner; the homeowner will have ten working days to request a hearing.

If the inspector decides that some corrective action is required by the contractor, the contractor and homeowner will be notified of the issues the inspector feels must be resolved. The contractor will have fifteen calendar days to comply, and either the contractor or homeowner may request an administrative hearing.

According to the Registrar of Contractors, most complaints are resolved without an administrative hearing. But an administrative hearing is required for any discipline to be levied against the contractor. (Such discipline generally results from a contractor's failure to comply with the order for corrective action.)

COMPLAINT PROCEDURES IN CALIFORNIA

In California, the Contractors State Licensing Board handles complaints stemming from the following behavior by contractors:

- Failure of a licensed contractor to fulfill the terms of an agreement, including poor workmanship
- Requiring a down payment in excess of 10 percent of the contract price, or in excess of $1,000
- Abandonment
- Failure to pay subcontractors, material suppliers, or employees
- Building code violations
- Use of false, misleading, or deceptive advertising
- Violations of home improvement contract requirements

When it receives a complaint, the Board's first step is to try to settle the matter, including through the use of arbitration. If the Board can't reach a settlement, then it may begin legal action, which starts with a citation against the contractor and ends with a referral to the attorney general for suspension or revocation of the contractor's license. However, the Board specifically advises homeowners that "there is no assurance that action will result in restitution. If a consumer's primary goal is to gain restitution, he or she should contact an attorney or the small claims court."

California's process is more complicated than Arizona's, but the initial steps taken are the same once the parties fail to reach a settlement: the complaint is assigned to an enforcement representative for investigation; then, if a workmanship or other performance violation is found, the contractor may be given a chance to fix the problem, or the board may issue a citation to the contractor. The citation may include a civil penalty, an order for restitution, an order of correction, or all three. If the contractor doesn't comply, the contractor's license can be suspended and the case referred to the attorney general's office, which can then start legal action to suspend or revoke the license.

RECOVERY FUNDS

Homeowner recovery funds or **guaranty funds** are state programs to compensate homeowners for losses caused by negligent or dishonest contractors. Most of these programs are funded by contractors' license fees. Homeowner recovery funds don't exist in every state, but in those states that have them, homeowners have at least the possibility of receiving some compensation for their losses. As is always the case, each state has different requirements that homeowners must meet in order to qualify for payment from the fund.

In Maryland, for instance, the Guaranty Fund "compensates homeowners for actual losses due to poor workmanship or failure to perform a home improvement contract by licensed contractors." In Virginia, a homeowner who claims breach of contract by the contractor is not eligible for compensation from the Contractor Transaction Recovery Fund. Instead, recovery in that state is limited to losses due to "improper or dishonest conduct," which includes theft, fraud, gross negligence, and "continued incompetence," but specifically excludes breach of contract. Florida requires a contractor's conduct to have caused financial harm to the homeowner.

In Virginia, the homeowner must have a court judgment against the contractor before filing a claim with the recovery fund. And in Massachusetts, a homeowner is only eligible to apply for compensation from the guaranty fund if he or she wins an award in arbitration or a judgment in court that the contractor fails to pay. Arizona allows the homeowner to apply directly to the fund if the contractor's license has been suspended or revoked; if not, the homeowner needs to sue the contractor and get a court order that directs the fund to pay toward the judgment.

In all of these states, recovery or guaranty funds are funded by the states' contractor license fees. This method of funding is great for the average taxpayer, but it also forces the states to set limits on the amount an individual homeowner can recover, and to limit the total amount that can be recovered against each contractor. Just to provide a sense of how these funds work, here are some limits placed on recovery in a few of the states:

 TALKING TO A LAWYER

Q. We signed a contract with a contractor to have a bedroom added to our house. We gave him $10,000 as a deposit. He came by and dropped off lumber the day before the job was supposed to start, but he hasn't been back since, and it's been over two months now. I called his office, but it's apparently closed. What do I do now? Is there someone to whom I can report this? Can I get my money back?

A. Contact a lawyer, your local licensing agency, and the state. See if there is a recovery fund and find out how to qualify for compensation.

—Answer by R. Stephen Hansell, lawyer, patent attorney, and construction arbitrator, Florence, Montana

- Maryland: $100,000 per contractor; $15,000 per homeowner
- Virginia: $40,000 per contractor per year; $10,000 per homeowner. If the total amount of claims against a single contractor exceeds $40,000, then the claim amounts are prorated.
- Massachusetts: $10,000 per homeowner
- Florida: $50,000 per homeowner
- Arizona: $200,000 per contractor; $30,000 per homeowner

In attempting to recover from a state recovery or guaranty fund, the length of the claims process will certainly be one of the homeowner's concerns. In Virginia, recovery fund claims are heard three or four days each year, and the Board of Contractors meets every six weeks to review the recommendations. In Massachusetts, a claim must be filed within six months of the award or judgment, and the claimant must prove that "all reasonable efforts to collect the judgment have been exhausted," which the state acknowledges may actually take longer than six months. In Arizona, the time frame for distributing money without a hearing is sixteen weeks. In short, the money is out there, and you may have a good chance of receiving some compensation—but don't hold your breath.

 ## CONTRACTOR'S LICENSE BOND

In the event of misconduct by a contractor, another avenue for homeowner compensation is the license bond that a contractor is required to post with the state when he or she becomes licensed. The bond, which ranges from $1,000 to $15,000 in most states, does not constitute a "deep pocket," but it can be another resource for satisfying a court judgment. When you file a lawsuit with the intent of going after the contractor's license bond, notify the state board in order to prevent the bond from being refunded to the contractor before you have a shot at it. You should also make sure that the court specifies that its judgment may be satisfied from the bond.

STATE AND LOCAL
CONSUMER PROTECTION

Every state today has a consumer protection statute prohibiting deceptive acts and practices. In addition, many states now have laws, or sections of consumer protection laws, specifically directed at the home renovation business.

In many of these states, "consumer fraud" is defined quite broadly in the context of residential contractors. As a result, some misconduct that might only have resulted in the loss of a license in the past can now expose contractors to serious financial liability, both from lawsuits by homeowners under state consumer fraud laws, and from separate lawsuits by state attorneys general. For example, several states have enacted consumer fraud laws that characterize a contractor's abandonment of a job as fraud. In Illinois, examples of consumer fraud include any deception or false promise, and a contractor can be found liable in a civil lawsuit even if the homeowner did not rely on the contractor's promises. In some states, even an innocent misrepresentation may be considered fraudulent. This expansion of the definition of "fraud" narrows the contractor's ability to avoid fraud charges, and that's very important for homeowners.

Some states that target dishonest contractors have gone even further and have made a contractor's violation of consumer fraud laws a crime. In Massachusetts, a contract for home improvement costing more than $1,000 must be in writing; the start date and completion date of the project must be in the contract; and the contract must also include a "detailed description" of the work, the total amount to be paid, and the schedule of payments. The Massachusetts definition of "deceptive practices" by contractors includes contracting beyond the scope of the contractor's registration (for example, performing plumbing work if the contractor is not a licensed plumber), abandonment of the project, and acting as an agent for a mortgage lender. A contractor who violates this law can be fined $2,000 and can be sentenced to one year in jail.

NEW JERSEY'S CONSUMER FRAUD ACT

New Jersey's Consumer Fraud Act provides as follows:

1. A contract for services of more than $200 must be in writing, and all change orders must also be in writing.

2. All the work and all the materials to be used in the project must be identified in writing.

3. The total project price, including finance charges, and all terms and conditions that affect the price, must be clearly described in writing.

4. Start and completion dates must be stated in writing; the contractor must supply the homeowner with a timely written notice of any delay, reasons for delay, and the new schedule.

5. The contractor must provide written warranties for any products, materials, labor, and other services he or she provides.

6. If the contractor violates the Consumer Fraud Act, the contract is void and the contractor is no longer entitled to be paid.

7. If the homeowner suffers property damage or loses money due to contractor violations, the contractor must pay triple the amount of the homeowner's damages.

8. A homeowner who files a Consumer Fraud Act complaint and can show that a violation has occurred is entitled to be reimbursed for attorney's fees.

The main focus of consumer fraud laws and consumer protection divisions is what might be called "classic fraud": con artists bilking homeowners, especially the disabled or the elderly, out of money. The most common predatory tactics include high-pressure sales, charging premium prices for low-quality materials; misrepresenting the need for repairs, and deceptive pricing.

At first glance, these types of deceptive practices seem almost too transparent to be successful. After all, what homeowner is going to pay cash to some guy who knocks on the door wanting to fix something the homeowner didn't know was broken? But the fact is, scams of this type are a serious problem. According to the Consumer Federation of America and the National Association of Consumer Agency Administrators, complaints about home improvement scams rose 23 percent nationwide in 2002, to a total of 300,000. Time after time, in county after county, prosecutors file home renovation fraud actions against local contractors who either took deposit money and failed to show up for work, or—probably worse—showed up for work and walked away without completing the job. These are crimes, period. Even where there is little chance of actually receiving restitution, the victim of a con artist or a contractor who abandons a job and refuses to return payments should contact the local police and the attorney general's office.

Bear in mind that the job of an attorney general, as with the police, is to enforce the law. This means that the law has to be broken—that is, a homeowner has to have been defrauded—before the state can take action. Even then, the focus is on catching and prosecuting the criminal, which prevents other homeowners from being victimized, but doesn't get the homeowner's lost money back.

HOME RENOVATION FRAUD IS A BIG DEAL

Don't think your case is too small, or just too embarrassing, to warrant bothering the state attorney general. According to the American Association of Retired Persons, more than 80 percent of cases of home renovation fraud committed against the elderly involve amounts of $5,000 or less. If you think the attorney general will brush you off, think again. The Illinois attorney general reports that of more than 20,000 complaints received annually by her office, 20 percent involve disputes between homeowners and home repair contractors.

FEDERAL CONSUMER PROTECTIONS

The most important consumer protection for homeowners under federal law is the Truth in Lending Act, which requires all lenders to state in writing the credit terms of a loan, and also gives a borrower three days to rescind the contract without penalty. Because the Truth in Lending Act applies everywhere, every lender is aware of it and is liable for drawing up a loan without the required disclosures. Chapter 1 contains more information about this act.

Federal law provides a couple of other protections for homeowners. The federal Consumer Protection Act sets out minimum requirements for written warranties on materials, both in terms of what must be disclosed to the consumer, and in terms of the minimum standards that must be met when replacing defective materials. The seller of materials must disclose what parts of a product are under warranty, what the company will do in the event of a defect or failure to conform with the guarantee (and at whose expense), and how long the warranty lasts. This means that all the materials used in and on your home are covered by some kind of warranty. And, under federal law, if the seller of those materials cannot remedy its defective product "after a reasonable number of attempts," you can elect to have the defective materials replaced at no charge, or to receive a full refund.

Federal Trade Commission rules also cover false advertising. "False advertising" generally refers to: (1) a seller advertising a product or service for less than what it really costs; or (2) a seller using a "bait-and-switch" tactic, in which a product or service is advertised, but the consumer who tries to buy it is told that the product isn't available, and instead is steered toward a more expensive product. A homeowner may encounter false advertising when shopping for roofing materials, kitchen and bathroom fixtures, or even quality lumber. The key word to watch for in this context is "available": watch out, for example, if a seller indicates that an item is "not *available* right now . . . it could be a month or two before it's back in stock." If you hear a phrase like that, at the very least you should inquire further. If you think you're

TALKING TO A LAWYER

Q. My elderly mother lives in a mobile-home park. Someone came to her door last week and told her that her roof needed to be fixed and offered to do the work. What should she do?

A. Check them out and get a second opinion.

—Answer by R. Stephen Hansell, lawyer, patent attorney, and construction arbitrator, Florence, Montana

being subjected to false advertising, then it's time for a serious conversation with the contractor, in which you let him or her know that you smell a bait-and-switch.

Unfortunately, you probably can't scare your contractor into behaving by threatening to complain to the FTC. The reason is that the FTC is concerned with eliminating consumer fraud, but it can only do so on a regional or national level; it will not intervene in individual cases of fraud. But although it might not help you personally, you can still file a consumer fraud complaint with the FTC either in writing, on the phone, or electronically through its website. Your complaint will be entered into its Consumer Sentinel database, which is linked to law enforcement agencies around the country. Using this database is a way for the FTC and law enforcement officials to spot trends on a regional, national, and even international level. And although the FTC cannot help with individual cases, its website contains educational information about consumer fraud schemes and financial issues that you may be dealing with in home renovation.

THE WORLD AT YOUR FINGERTIPS

• For more information on your state's regulation of contractors, go to your state government's website and search for "contractors." If your state has a licensing agency, you probably will be able to search for information about contractors you are considering for your renovation. If the agency doesn't provide the information on its website, it most likely will have a phone number you can call for that information. The extent of the information available will vary from state to state, but at the very least you should be able to find out whether a contractor is licensed; you may also be able to find out if the contractor is bonded and whether previous complaints have been filed with the agency.

• Your state attorney general's website may have a great deal of information about home renovation issues; if it doesn't, it should have information about consumer protection and fraud issues, many of which carry over to home renovation.

REMEMBER THIS

• All states have consumer protection laws and many of them include tough laws aimed at fraud and misconduct by contractors.

• Your state licensing board has the power to put a contractor out of business; that makes the board your first stop with a formal complaint against a contractor.

• If your state does not regulate contractors at the state level, contact your county or municipality for issues relating to licensing or regulating of contractors. Many counties and cities require contractors to pass a competency examination in order to obtain a license.

• Many states now have homeowner recovery funds that can provide some amount of financial relief for homeowner losses due to contractor misconduct or fraud.

CHAPTER 9

The Role of a Lawyer

Finding Help When You Need It

Jim and Emily became worried that their renovation was falling apart. The contractor hadn't shown up for weeks, and the job was barely half done. It seemed to be time to call in a lawyer, but neither of them knew a lawyer or had ever been to a lawyer's office.

Emily called a lawyer who was recommended by a friend of a next-door neighbor. She was surprised to get straight through to the lawyer on her first call, and she was even more surprised to find that the lawyer could see them the next day—and that there would be no fee for a half-hour consultation. The lawyer told them to bring all the paperwork associated with the renovation so that she could get a quick idea of the situation.

When Jim and Emily went to the lawyer's office, they waited a few minutes in a small waiting room before the lawyer came out and led them into her office. She sat down behind her desk, smiled, and got right to it. "So, tell me what's going on with you and your contractor."

You probably have certain expectations of a lawyer and what a lawyer can do for you. Those expectations may be based on experience, but chances are they are based on friends' stories or television. This chapter will give you some authoritative information on how you can go about finding a suitable lawyer; the questions you should ask him or her at your first meeting; and how you can help keep a lid on costs.

WHEN TO HIRE A LAWYER

It's important to understand that a lawyer does not have a time machine. The lawyer has to deal with your situation as it exists now, not as you wish it were. So if your contractor walked off the job two months ago, there's nothing the lawyer can do to recover those two months. Which is why the sooner you see a lawyer, the better. Working to undo problems that have already occurred can be time-consuming, expensive, and futile for you and the lawyer.

It's a good idea to hire or at least consult with a lawyer when you start your project, before you sign a contract, and well before any trouble starts brewing. If you already have a contract, the lawyer can read it and give you the good and bad news about it— that is, what protections the contract provides for you, and what protections it should provide but doesn't. It's possible that parts of your contract are illegal or fail to meet state requirements, such as the requirement that a contractor present a statement of adequate insurance coverage. Deficiencies in your contract could mean that it has to be renegotiated. Even if there's nothing wrong with your contract, a lawyer—especially one who specializes in construction or real estate law—can tell you what to expect as the project moves along, what trouble spots to watch out for, and what the contractor owes you in terms of workmanship, adhering to the schedule, and minimizing your inconvenience. An added bonus is that if you talk to a lawyer at an early stage, before the project runs into trouble, you're not going to be angry and frustrated, so you will be able to think clearly about what you want and need.

If you have a lawyer who is familiar with your situation from the beginning, he or she can take steps quickly to prevent a small problem from turning into a big problem. If, for instance, you're starting to have trouble with your contractor, a lawyer can explain to you what your legal position is, what the contractor's legal position is, and give you advice on how to deal with the contractor. That may mean keeping notes on the progress of the job, or sitting the contractor down and walking through the contract again to clarify responsibilities and obligations, or simply schmoozing with the contractor. Or the lawyer might write a letter to the contractor, putting the contractor on notice that if the situation worsens you're prepared to take legal action. Either way, you aren't stuck in the corner, wringing your hands over your contractor problems as they start to spin out of control; you're taking positive steps to keep the project going. If you wait to talk to a lawyer until the contractor walks off the job and threatens to slap a mechanic's lien on your property, you could find yourself facing more complex legal problems and fewer options for resolution.

A lawyer can also be a good sounding board for a worried homeowner. You don't want to waste your lawyer's time with minor complaints and fears (and pay the fees for it), but a lawyer can listen to your problems and tell you what's worth worrying about and what isn't, and what can be done or can't be done. And the lawyer, looking ahead to possible litigation, can also instruct you on how to stay on the side of the angels so that you remain relatively blameless in the dispute. If you have to go to court, you don't want to have done things that a judge sees as having interfered with the contractor's ability to do the job.

Finally, if the situation has deteriorated to the point at which you're headed for arbitration or court, you will need a lawyer to take charge. Though it's possible to handle an arbitration without a lawyer, it's not a good idea for at least two reasons: first, the contractor will more than likely have a lawyer; and second, even though arbitration is less formal than court, there are still rules to follow and legal strategies to pursue. You'll need a lawyer to serve your best interests.

 A FOOL FOR A CLIENT

Should you represent yourself in an arbitration or lawsuit? The short answer is "no." Even lawyers don't represent themselves. The old adage is, "A lawyer who represents himself has a fool for a client." The world of the law is not a place for amateurs. It is a place best negotiated by an expert, who can also take an objective view of the case.

The exception is if you're going to small-claims court, where lawyers are either not allowed to represent you at all, or are restricted in their involvement.

HOW DO YOU FIND A LAWYER?

It's a cliché, but it's true: There's no substitute for experience. Look for a lawyer who has represented homeowners in home renovation cases. That's the starting point. One advantage in dealing with an experienced lawyer is that he or she has likely seen very similar situations and can estimate quickly what the potential problems are, what the likely outcome will be, and how much time your case will take.

You can find a lawyer in much the same way that you find a contractor: ask around. If you know a couple of lawyers, ask them for recommendations (one lawyer recommending another is a sign of professional respect, so you definitely should follow up on any lawyer referrals). You can also ask friends who have been through similar homeowner agonies for recommendations. To find a lawyer who specializes in real estate or construction law—if you don't know any lawyers—your best bets are bar associations. Most state bar associations have sections for real estate and construction law specialists, and the American Bar Association has two specialty sections for lawyers who have an understanding of home renovation issues: the Real Property, Probate, and Trust Law Section, and the Construction Industry Forum. In most communities you can find county or city bar-sponsored lawyer referral services. Often these services maintain specialty panels to help you find lawyers who have experience in residential renovation and contracting issues. The ABA maintains an online directory of lawyer referral services at *www.abanet.org/legalservices/lris/directory.html*.

Since many lawyers now advertise their practice areas, simply by looking in the Yellow Pages you should be able to locate a number of lawyers in your area who practice in real estate or construction law. Be aware, though, that only seven states certify lawyers as specialists in real estate and only one, Florida, certifies lawyers as construction law specialists. So in most states, the credentials that lawyers advertise (such as concentration of practice in real estate or construction law) may be self-

THE MARTINDALE-HUBBELL LEGAL DIRECTORY

The Martindale-Hubbell Legal Directory contains background information on most lawyers based on information provided by the lawyers themselves. Included in this network is information about each lawyer's education, experience, services, and fields of practice. Many firms also list their most important clients. Lawyers are rated "AV," "BV," and "CV" based on confidential opinions from other lawyers and judges. Just as in grade school, "A" is better than "B," and so on. You can find copies of Martindale-Hubbell online at *www.abanet.org/premartindale.html* or in most law libraries. Not all lawyers are listed in Martindale-Hubbell, and the absence of a listing should not be held against a lawyer.

proclaimed, without independent verification. Keep in mind, too, that you will not need your state's best real estate attorney to represent you in a $5,000 dispute.

The truth is, it's not hard to find a lawyer to handle your case. Once you have a few names, pick up the phone and make some appointments. Talk to different lawyers until you find one with whom you're comfortable. And, if you ask, most lawyers will give you the names and telephone numbers of a couple of satisfied clients whom you can call for a reference.

WHAT QUESTIONS TO ASK

No matter what the areas in which a lawyer says he or she concentrates, it's best to verify for yourself whether he or she will be able to meet your needs. During your first phone call, ask the attorney or the attorney's secretary or office manager the following questions:

1. How long has the lawyer been in practice?
2. What percentage of the lawyer's practice is devoted to

real estate or construction law, and has he or she handled home renovation cases?

3. If the lawyer is a specialist in real estate or construction law, how long has the attorney specialized? What specialty memberships or certifications does he or she have?

4. Can the lawyer provide you with references to clients with similar needs whom he or she has served?

5. Is there a fee for the first consultation, and if so, how much is it?

6. If you make an appointment, what information should you bring with you to the initial consultation?

Many lawyers will have no problem talking with you for half an hour without charge, but you will have to respect the lawyer's time, so come prepared to summarize the facts of your situation briefly and accurately (a written summary can be helpful). You ought to be able to explain your situation in less than ten minutes—if you need to practice beforehand, then do so. Park your anger outside the office and don't get bogged down in minute details or the personality quirks of the contractor. Holding your summary to ten minutes will give the lawyer plenty of time to ask you questions and to explain what steps need to be taken, what alternatives you may have, and what the possible outcomes are. You should also expect the lawyer to discuss fees with you—the hourly rate, an estimate of the cost, and whether he or she expects a retainer. A **retainer** is a lump sum you pay when you hire the lawyer. Your fees will be taken out of the retainer until it's used up; if the case closes with some of the retainer left over, that amount will be refunded to you. Some lawyers are reluctant to be very specific with a cost estimate, because situations can change drastically, but the lawyer ought to be able to provide you with a best-case/worst-case scenario.

When you talk with a lawyer about your case, ask if he or she will be directly working on the case. This is neither an insult nor an idle question. If the lawyer is in a small firm, more than likely he or she will be doing all the work on the case and will be the person you talk to all the time. As law firms get larger, the part-

ARE YOU COMFORTABLE WITH THIS PERSON?

When you're making your hiring decision, don't forget to take into account your comfort level with each attorney you're considering. This might be a matter of personal style or personality, physical environment, office organization and staffing, and convenience (convenient office hours, availability by phone). You want to feel comfortable confiding in your lawyer, and you want to feel that he or she will return your calls promptly and will be able to give you the time and attention you want.

ners' workload is shared with younger members of the firm (**associates**) and with **paralegals**, highly trained non-lawyers who assist in research and case preparation. Upon taking the case, the lawyer usually will tell you how the work will be structured and will introduce you to the associate and paralegal who will be assigned to the case. But if the lawyer doesn't talk about how the work will be divided, you should ask. If it's a large firm, most of your dealings are likely to be with the associate, and with the partner supervising the case.

The more work an associate does (as opposed to a more-experienced, more-expensive partner), the lower your fees will be. If you're going with a large law firm, you shouldn't be put off by having the more mundane aspects of your case assigned to associates and paralegals—that's just the way large firms do business. Keep in mind, too, that associates are likely to be skilled lawyers—in fact, they may have a great deal of expertise. They just haven't accumulated enough gray hair to become partners.

FEES

Most lawyers charge by the hour, but there is no standard per-hour charge for legal services. In general, a large firm in a large city will charge more than a small firm in a small town. Generally, the more experience a lawyer has, the higher his or her per-hour fee. But that doesn't necessarily mean you'll spend more if you hire a more experienced lawyer; because of his or her greater expertise, a more experienced lawyer may be able to complete the legal work involved in far fewer hours, and for a lower total fee, than a less experienced lawyer.

Many lawyers charge more for courtroom time than for office time, based on the assumption that courtroom work requires more skill and more pressure than office work. If work can be handled by a paralegal or other staff person, then the billing rate will be less for that work. And keep in mind that you will probably incur costs in addition to the lawyer's fees (see the sidebar below for more information).

Contingent-fee arrangements—in which a lawyer takes a percentage of the settlement or judgment, rather than charging an hourly fee—are generally limited to personal injury cases and to cases of fraud. Most home renovation cases will be breach-of-contract cases, which means that your fees will probably be calculated on an hourly basis.

How much will it cost? Naturally, it depends on the nature of the legal help you need—whether you just need a lawyer to give you advice before you sign a contract, or whether your dispute is going to court and you need a lawyer to handle the litigation. But whatever the nature of your case, there are several ways in which you can keep a lid on legal fees.

Don't Waste Time

Remember that you are being charged money every time you talk to your lawyer—whether in person or on the phone—so it's not a good idea, or at least not a cost-effective one, to consult your lawyer over trivial matters. Keep your phone calls or visits short and to the point. Don't chatter about the basketball game. Don't call your lawyer to blow off steam—it's not a good use of the lawyer's time or your money. It's better to save up several questions for one phone call than to pepper your lawyer with a series of five-minute calls. When your lawyer takes your call, he or she has probably taken a few minutes to scan your file to get up to speed; it's much more efficient to have him or her do that every couple of weeks than five times in two weeks.

Replying right away to your lawyer's requests for information will also help reduce billable time. Don't waste money making your lawyer follow up on requests or correct errors caused by your incomplete answers to requests for information.

As a client, you have to understand that lawyers cannot always take your calls. Lawyers, particularly successful ones, are very busy meeting with other clients and arguing in court. A well-organized lawyer will usually return calls within a day or so,

 WHAT ARE THE ADDITIONAL COSTS?

When you hire a lawyer, in addition to lawyer's fees, you will be responsible for some additional costs, including:

- Court filing fees (fees paid to the court for filing a lawsuit or filing a response to a lawsuit)
- Process server fees (the **process server** is the person who delivers legal papers to the opposing side)
- Subpoena fees (fees paid to persons ordered to appear in court or to deliver documents to a party)
- Court reporter fees (fees paid to the reporter who records depositions and provides written transcripts. A **deposition** is a procedure in which a lawyer questions a party or witness under oath; it usually takes place in a lawyer's office.)
- Telephone, fax, mailing, and photocopying expenses
- Travel expenses
- Fees to experts (depending on your case, you may need expert testimony on the quality of workmanship, standard industry practices, safety issues, and so on.)

or arrange to have a staff member return your call. When you meet with your lawyer early on, you should develop an understanding about the best way for you to communicate. Find out if there is a time when the lawyer prefers to take calls, when he or she generally returns calls (many lawyers will put off returning calls until the late afternoon), or if the lawyer prefers e-mail for non-emergency questions.

Be Prepared

Well-prepared clients can help their cases go more smoothly. Clients can save time and money by gathering facts and carefully considering what goals they want to achieve. When you consult a lawyer, be prepared to answer the question: what do you want? The lawyer's job is to get you the best result, but you can help to define what that result should be. If you want the contractor to go away and never return, then the lawyer has certain options; if you want the contractor to get back to work and finish the job, the lawyer might pursue different options.

One way for you to keep the lawyer's hours in check is to be organized. Organize your notes (preferably chronologically), and make sure they are clearly written so that the lawyer can determine quickly how each note is significant.

Hire a Lawyer for a Limited Purpose

When you are seeking legal help, keep in mind that it is not always necessary to hire a lawyer for full-scale representation. You can hire a lawyer for a limited purpose. For example, at the beginning or in the middle of a dispute, you can hire a lawyer simply to give advice or review a document. You can pay a lawyer for consultations in which you explain the facts of your case and seek the lawyer's advice about your rights, additional steps you will need to take, and the likely outcome of the case. You then can tailor your plans for handling the case based on the perspectives gained from the lawyer. Using a lawyer for a limited purpose rather than for full-scale representation is sometimes referred to as **unbundling** legal services.

You can also hire a lawyer for the purpose of negotiating a settlement, without committing to hire the lawyer for a long, expensive trial. And if it looks like you're heading for a full-scale trial, you may want to consider hiring another lawyer—not for full representation, but to provide a second opinion. Just as patients often want a second opinion before undertaking major medical treatment, it can be prudent to seek a second legal opinion before taking a major legal action that could affect your life for years to come.

 WHAT RECORDS SHOULD YOU KEEP?

You should keep a file with all papers related to your home improvement job, including:

- The contract and any change orders
- Plans and specifications
- Bills and invoices
- Cancelled checks
- All correspondence with the contractor
- Any notes you made during conversations with the contractor
- Lien releases from subcontractors and material suppliers
- A record sheet on each subcontractor listing the work performed and the length of time he or she has spent on the job
- Warranties
- Samples, swatches, or identifying information on materials used in your project
- Photographs, videos, progress reports, and inspection reports

EVALUATING YOUR LAWYER

How do you know your lawyer is doing a good job representing you? If the lawyer understands your situation and lets you know that he or she has your best interests in mind, you're on the right track. The bottom line, of course, is whether you are getting the results you are entitled to, which may not be what you wanted. Part of a lawyer's job is to educate you about what your realistic expectations in your case should be. But remember: the sooner you bring in the lawyer, the better the job he or she can do for you. Sometimes, if the lawyer is brought in after disaster has already struck you and your home, the best the lawyer can do is clean up after the parade.

How do you know if a lawyer is not representing you well? For one thing, your lawyer should return your phone calls. Some lawyers are better than others at returning calls promptly, but they all should return calls from clients. If you can't reach your lawyer, or you find that you don't have a good idea of what's going on in your case, then you are not being well served by your lawyer. If you're not important enough for your lawyer to talk to, then you should find another lawyer. If your lawyer seems disorganized (don't assume too much from the appearance of disorganization in a lawyer's office—a messy office does not necessarily indicate a messy mind) or has a difficult time remembering details about your case, you might want to think about talking to another lawyer. Successful lawyers have dozens of active cases and have no problem juggling the demands of each case—that ability is one of the reasons for their success.

If the case seems to be stumbling along, with a lot of delays, court dates rescheduled, depositions canceled, and a general lack of progress, you should talk to your lawyer. The legal process is slow and frustrating under most circumstances, but there should always be progress toward a trial or settlement; if your lawyer seems content to let your case languish, again, you're not being well served. A good lawyer will let you know

HONESTY IS THE BEST POLICY

Be sure to be completely honest with your lawyer. Lawyers spend many hours a day listening to clients with embarrassing things to admit, and are required to hold in confidence whatever they are told by their clients. So if you have done something stupid or dishonest, let the lawyer know. You're not in the lawyer's office to look as good as possible; you're there to be honest, complete, and direct so that the lawyer can assess your case properly. Every case has strengths and every case has weaknesses. If your lawyer doesn't discover the weakness in your case until the middle of a negotiation or trial, the lawyer may have to react without time to prepare an effective response to the disclosure.

what you're in for at the start—litigation is never smooth, but a good lawyer will control what he or she can in order to keep the case moving, and will tell you (though you might have to ask) what delays he or she can't control.

THE WORLD AT YOUR FINGERTIPS

- For help in finding a lawyer, visit your county or state bar association's website. If the site lists lawyers by specialty area, look for lawyers who specialize in real estate or construction law. You can find links to your local or state bar association on the American Bar Association website at *www.abanet.org/barserv/stlobar.html*.
- The ABA also offers a lawyer referral service at *www.abanet.org/legalservices/findlegalhelp*.
- The following states certify lawyers as specialists in real estate law: Arizona, Florida, Minnesota, New Mexico, North Carolina, Ohio, and Texas. Only Florida certifies lawyers as construction law specialists.

REMEMBER THIS

- The more that's at stake—in terms of both money and risk—the more likely you are to need legal help.

- Early help is better than late help; after you've signed a contract, your lawyer might not be able to do much for you.

- Personal recommendations from people you trust are a good way to find a good lawyer.

- Recommendations from people who have used a lawyer in home renovation or construction issues are especially desirable.

- Try to interview several lawyers before you retain one, and ask each one the same questions: about experience, availability, and fees.

- A lawyer charges you for his or her time; there might be a great deal you can make to reduce the time your lawyer spends on your case, and thus reduce your total costs.

CHAPTER 10

Where Do You Go From Here?

Throughout this book, we've provided you with resources for finding more information on a variety of topics associated with home renovation. You can build on your knowledge by checking out the following websites and books, and following up on other helpful suggestions in this chapter. Some of these resources may have been mentioned earlier; we think they're your best places to start.

THE KITCHEN SINK: 8 WEBSITES TO GET YOU STARTED

Remodeling a home takes work—whether you've hired a contractor, are doing it yourself, or are just beginning to think about it—but finding helpful information is easy with the following websites. These sites cover everything from zoning laws to installing appliances to health concerns (e.g., mold, asbestos, and lead). Some of these websites are housed within larger sites, but contain lengthy sections on topics associated with home renovation. You're bound to find what you're looking for at one of these sites, or from one of their links. (Note: These are not arranged in any order of preference.)

National Association of the Remodeling Industry—*www .nari.org*
Click on "Home Owners" for information and articles on finding contractors, remodeling tips, frequently asked questions, and more.

Hometime.com—*www.hometime.com*

Site of the television show *Hometime*, which airs nationally on public television and cable stations. Click on "How-to" for links to product manufacturers and a wealth of information about do-it-yourself projects, resources, safety, and much more.

DannyLipford.com—*www.dannylipford.com*
Danny Lipford, a remodeling contractor and host of the television show *Today's Homeowner with Danny Lipford*, offers a site chock-full of information about all things home improvement. Click on "Home Improvement" for articles about avoiding scams, working with contractors, tackling remodeling jobs, financial matters (including contracts), and more.

U.S. Department of Housing and Urban Development (HUD)—*www.hud.gov*
Click on "Home Improvements" for information about federal loans, community programs, and more. This site is also available in Spanish.

National Association of Home Builders—*www.nahb.org*
Click "Resources," then "For Consumers," then "Remodeling Your Home" to access information about remodeling your home. Articles include tips on financing your project, finding and hiring professional remodelers, coping with project-related stress, being a good neighbor, and more.

FirstGov for Consumers—*www.consumer.gov*
This government site features information about home improvements and some quizzes to test your knowledge about hiring a contractor and other related topics. Click on "Home & Community" to get started. This site features links to other government websites, including those of the Federal Trade Commission, the Environmental Protection Agency, and HUD.

ImproveNet—*www.improvenet.com*
This comprehensive site includes everything you need to know about the remodeling process. The site features a down-

loadable project-planning guide, articles written by architects and other experts, information on loans, liens, and insurance, and much more. Click on "Resources" to get started.

Environmental Protection Agency—*www.epa.gov*
Topics addressed on this website include indoor air quality (including information about mold, radon, and asbestos) and a section about lead. This site also features downloadable pamphlets (some available in Spanish) and links to further information.

ADD TO YOUR LIBRARY: BOOKS WORTH THEIR SHELF SPACE

Find a home on your bookshelf for these books on remodeling and home improvement. But don't stop with these; you can find many more at your local library, as well as at Amazon.com and other online bookstores.

What the Experts May Not Tell You about Building or Renovating Your Home *by Amy Johnston. Warner Books (April 2004).*

THE Survival Guide: Home Remodeling *by Diane Plesset. D. P. Design Publishing (September 2003).*

Renovating Old Houses (For Pros By Pros Series) *by George Nash. Taunton (October 1998).*

On Time and On Budget: A Home Renovation Survival Guide *by John Rusk. Main Street Books (Reprint Edition, May 1997).*

Before You Hire a Contractor: A Construction Guidebook for Consumers *by Steve Gonzalez. Consumer Press (November 1999).*

DON'T FORGET . . .

Check local venues for courses, lectures and seminars, and expert panels related to real estate, including those addressing various associated topics such as finance, insurance, contracts, and so on. Start with your local library, bar association, area colleges, and senior citizens' centers to see what's in the works, or even to suggest a topic for upcoming events. Local radio and television stations may also feature experts on real estate law and home improvement, so get with the programs. Don't forget that there's a plethora of home improvement shows on many cable networks (as well as on public and local channels). Many of these programs also have websites that offer a variety of resources. And your local newspaper's real estate section might also include tips and tricks relating to financing, working with contractors, and consumer protection laws.

The Internet is also a great resource. Countless message boards, user groups, mailing lists, and chat rooms exist in cyberspace; many of these could help you in your quest for knowledge and provide a "been there, done that" perspective on issues you're facing. Communicating with others who have been in your position is a great way of learning about other avenues to explore, and what pitfalls to avoid.

That's about all we have for you now. So without further redo, we invite you to begin checking out the resources above and wish you good luck with your project. We also welcome your comments and suggestions for future editions of this book. Please visit us on the Web at *www.abanet.org/publiced* or drop us a line via e-mail at: abapubed@abanet.org

APPENDIX

State Licensing Boards, Consumer Protection Agencies, and Additional Resources

Below is a list of state licensing boards and consumer protection agencies.

You should contact your state's licensing board when you are deciding whether to hire a particular contractor. Most boards maintain lists of licensed contractors, and some boards also make available any records of legal actions or complaints against contractors. If you are having trouble with your contractor, you should complain to the state licensing board, which in most states can discipline a contractor who is dishonest or incompetent.

Consumer protection agencies are primarily focused on fraud. But remember: in some states, many instances of contractor misconduct—including a contractor walking off the job—are considered fraud. So if you're having serious trouble with your contractor, complain to your state consumer protection agency in addition to your state's licensing board.

STATE CONTRACTOR LICENSING BOARDS AND CONSUMER PROTECTION AGENCIES

(Note that not all states require contractors to be licensed.)

ALABAMA
Home Builders Licensure Board
www.hblb.state.al.us

Consumer Information
www.hblb.state.al.us/consumer-info.html

Attorney General, Consumer Affairs
www.ago.state.al.us/consumer.cfm

ALASKA
Division of Occupational Licensing
*www.commerce.state.ak.us/occ/pcon
.htm*

Attorney General, Consumer Protection
*www.law.state.ak.us/department/civil/
consumer/cpindex.html*

ARIZONA
Registrar of Contractors
www.rc.state.az.us

Attorney General, Consumer Issues
www.azag.gov/consumer/index.html

ARKANSAS
Arkansas Contractors Licensing
Board
www.arkansas.gov/clb

Attorney General, Consumer Protection Division
www.arkansasag.gov/citserv/home.htm

CALIFORNIA
Contractors State License Board
www.cslb.ca.gov

Attorney General
www.ag.ca.gov

COLORADO
Department of Regulatory Agencies
www.dora.state.co.us

Attorney General, Consumer Protection
*www.ago.state.co.us/consumer_
protection.cfm?MenuPage=True*

CONNECTICUT
Department of Consumer
Protection, Home Improvement
*www.ct.gov/dcp/cwp/view.asp?a=
1625&Q=274440&dcpNav=|*

Attorney General, Consumer Issues
*www.cslib.org/attygenl/mainlinks/
tabindex3.htm*

DELAWARE
Department of Finance, Division of
Revenue
*www.state.de.us/revenue/information/
tims/Contractor.shtml*

Attorney General, Fraud/Consumer
Protection
*www.state.de.us/attgen/fraud/
consumerprotection/
consumerprotection.htm*

DISTRICT OF COLUMBIA
Business and Professional
Licensing Administration/
Occupational and Professional
Licensing Division
*dcra.dc.gov/dcra/cwp/view,a,1342,q,
600813,dcraNav_GID,1697,
dcraNav,|33466|.asp*

Department of Consumer and Regulatory Affairs
dcra.dc.gov/dcra/site/default.asp

FLORIDA
Department of Business and
Professional Regulation
www.state.fl.us/dbpr

Attorney General, Consumer Protection
myfloridalegal.com/consumer

GEORGIA
Business and Professional
    Licensing
www.georgia.gov/00/channel_title/0,
    2094,4802_5039,00.html

Governor's Office of Consumer
    Affairs
www.georgia.gov/02/oca/home/
    0,2471,5426814,00.html

HAWAII
Professional and Vocational
    Licensing Division
www.hawaii.gov/dcca/areas/pvl

Department of Commerce and
    Consumer Affairs, Office of
    Consumer Protection
www.hawaii.gov/dcca/areas/ocp

IDAHO
Professional Licensing
www.accessidaho.org/business/
    licensing.html

Attorney General, Consumer Pro-
    tection Unit
www2.state.id.us/ag/consumer/
    index.htm

ILLINOIS
Division of Professional Regulation
www.idfpr.com/dpr/default.asp

Attorney General, Consumer Pro-
    tection Division
www.ag.state.il.us/consumers/index
    .html

INDIANA
Licensing and Permits
www.in.gov/ai/licensing

Attorney General, Consumer
    Services
www.in.gov/attorneygeneral/consumer

IOWA
Division of Labor, Construction
    Contractor Registration/
    Bonding
www.iowaworkforce.org/labor/
    contractor.htm

Attorney General, Consumer Pro-
    tection Division
www.state.ia.us/government/ag/
    consumer/index.html

KANSAS
Attorney General, Consumer
    Protection Division
http://www.ksag.org/Divisions/
    Consumer/main.htm

KENTUCKY
Department of Housing, Buildings
    and Construction
hbc.ky.gov/licensing/electrical/
    license_lookup.asp

Attorney General, Consumer Pro-
    tection Division
ag.ky.gov/cp

LOUISIANA
State Licensing Board for
    Contractors, Residential
    Building Contractors
    Subcommittee
*www.legis.state.la.us/boards/board_*
    members.asp?board=502

Attorney General, Consumer
    Protection
www.ag.state.la.us/Consumers.aspx

MAINE
Attorney General, Home
  Construction/Repair
www.maine.gov/ag/index.php?r=
  protection&s=construction&t

MARYLAND
Department of Labor, Home
  Improvement Contractor,
  Subcontractor, and Salesperson
  License
www.blis.state.md.us/LicenseDetail.
  aspx?LicenseIDs=302

Attorney General, Consumer Protection Division
www.oag.state.md.us/Consumer/
  index.htm

MASSACHUSETTS
Board of Building Regulations and
  Standards
www.mass.gov/bbrs/programs.htm

Attorney General, Consumer
  Protection
www.ago.state.ma.us/sp.cfm?
  pageid=967

MICHIGAN
Business & Industry, Construction
  Licensing & Permits
www.michigan.gov/som/0,1607,
  7--192--29943_31469_31893---,
  00.html

Attorney General, Consumer
  Protection
www.michigan.gov/ag/0,1607,7--
  164--17334_17362----,00.html

MINNESOTA
Department of Labor & Industry,
  Construction Codes and
  Licensing Division
www.bizlinks.org/license.html

Attorney General, Consumer Protection Division
www.ag.state.mn.us/consumer/
  default.htm

MISSISSIPPI
State Board of Contractors
www.msboc.state.ms.us

Attorney General
www.ago.state.ms.us

MISSOURI
Attorney General, Consumer
  Protection Division
www.ago.mo.gov/divisions/
  consumerprotection.htm

MONTANA
Attorney General, Consumer
  Protection Office
www.doj.mt.gov/consumer

NEBRASKA
Nebraska Workforce Development,
  Safety, Labor Standards
www.dol.state.ne.us/nwd/center.cfm?
  PRICAT=2&SUBCAT=2C&
  ACTION=contractors

Attorney General, Consumer Protection Division
www.ago.state.ne.us

NEVADA
State Contractors Board
nscb.state.nv.us

Attorney General, Bureau of Consumer Protection
ag.state.nv.us/actionbutton/bcp/bcp.htm

NEW HAMPSHIRE
Attorney General, Consumer Protection & Antitrust Bureau
doj.nh.gov/consumer/index.html

NEW JERSEY
Home Improvement Contractors' Registration
www.state.nj.us/lps/ca/contractor.htm

Attorney General, Division of Consumer Affairs
www.state.nj.us/lps/ca/home.htm

NEW MEXICO
Regulation & Licensing Department, Construction Industries Division
www.rld.state.nm.us/CID/Wrkcontractor/wrkcontractor.htm

Attorney General, Consumer Protection
www.ago.state.nm.us/protectcons/protectcons.htm

NEW YORK
Attorney General, Bureau of Consumer Frauds and Protection
www.oag.state.ny.us/consumer/consumer_issues.html

NORTH CAROLINA
Licensing Board for General Contractors
www.nclbgc.com

Attorney General, Consumer Protection Division
www.ncdoj.com/consumerprotection/cp_about.jsp

NORTH DAKOTA
Secretary of State, Contractor Licensing
www.nd.gov/sos/licensing/

Attorney General, Consumer Protection and Antitrust Division
www.ag.state.nd.us/CPAT/CPAT.htm

OHIO
Attorney General, Consumer Protection Enforcement
www.ag.state.oh.us/citizen/consumer/index.asp

OKLAHOMA
Attorney General, Consumer Protection Division
www.oag.state.ok.us/oagweb.nsf/Consumer!OpenPage

OREGON
Construction Contractors Board
www.ccb.state.or.us/New_Web/contractors/new_contractors.htm

Attorney General, Financial Fraud/Consumer Protection
www.doj.state.or.us/FinFraud/welcome3.htm

PENNSYLVANIA
Attorney General, Bureau of
  Consumer Protection
*www.attorneygeneral.gov/consumers.
  aspx?id=255*

RHODE ISLAND
Contractors' Registration Board
www.crb.state.ri.us

Attorney General, Consumer Protection Unit
*www.riag.state.ri.us/civil/unit.php?
  name=consumer*

SOUTH CAROLINA
Contractors' Licensing Board
www.llr.state.sc.us/POL/Contractors/

Department of Consumer Affairs
www.scconsumer.gov

SOUTH DAKOTA
Attorney General, Consumer
  Protection Unit
*www.state.sd.us/attorney/office/
  divisions/consumer/default.asp*

TENNESSEE
Licensing Contractors Board
*www.tennessee.gov/commerce/boards/
  contractors/index.html*

Department of Commerce and Insurance, Division of Consumer
  Affairs
www.state.tn.us/consumer

TEXAS
Residential Construction
  Commission
*www.trcc.state.tx.us/faq/faq_build_
  reg.htm*

Attorney General, Consumer Protection and Public Health
*www.oag.state.tx.us/consumer/
  consumer.shtml*

UTAH
Construction Services
  Commission
*www.dopl.utah.gov/licensing/
  contractor.html*

Attorney General, Consumer
  Assistance
*www.attygen.state.ut.us/
  consumerassistance.html*

VERMONT
Attorney General, Consumer
  Protection Unit
*www.atg.state.vt.us/display.php?
  smod=8*

VIRGINIA
Board for Contractors
www.state.va.us/dpor/con_main.htm

Attorney General, Consumer
  Assistance
*www.oag.state.va.us/Protecting/
  Consumer%20Fraud/consumer_
  assistance.htm*

WASHINGTON
Department of Labor and
  Industries, Contractors
*www.lni.wa.gov/TradesLicensing/
  Contractors/default.asp*

Attorney General, Consumer Protection Program
*www.atg.wa.gov/consumerintro
  .shtml*

WEST VIRGINIA
Division of Labor, Contractor
    Licensing
www.labor.state.wv.us

Attorney General, Consumer Pro-
    tection Division
www.wvago.us

WISCONSIN
Attorney General, Office of
    Consumer Protection
*www.doj.state.wi.us/dls/ConsProt/
    newcp.asp*

WYOMING
Attorney General, Consumer
    Protection Unit
*attorneygeneral.state.wy.us/
    consumer.htm*

Throughout this book, we've given you resources to help you find more information on home renovation. Below we've listed some more resources for you to check. Read on for information about where you can find sample contracts; where you can find a lawyer, contractor, arbitrator, or mediator; and contact information for federal agencies and community associations.

SAMPLE CONTRACTS

A sample of a good home improvement contract would be too long to provide here. But there are some good examples of home improvement contracts online. Below are the Web addresses for two sample contracts written to meet requirements in California. While California's requirements for a home renovation contract are likely to be different from your state's specific requirements, the same general principles will apply. You can use these sample contracts as models, to remind you what issues you should address in your own contract.

*www.abag.ca.gov/bayarea/eqmaps/
    fixit/manual/PT20-App-G.PDF*

*www.cooperativecommunityenergy
    .com/resources/tools/Home_
    Improvement_Contract2.pdf*

The American Institute of Architects (AIA) provides examples of more than eighty standard contracts for homeowners, contractors, and architects. The contract forms cost between $5 and $10 each; visit *www.aia.org.*

Be aware that these are standard contracts and may not fit your situation exactly; however, a standard contract can serve as a model that you can revise to meet your specific needs. You certainly should talk to an attorney before using any of these contracts.

The California Contractors State License Board provides a checklist for contracts and examples of precise wording for certain clauses; visit *www.cslb.ca.gov/contractors/hicontracts.asp#2a.*

FIND A LAWYER

As we noted in chapter 9, state and local bar associations are excellent resources for finding a lawyer who specializes in real estate or construction law. Here are two national sources that you can use to find lawyers in your area:

American Bar Association
www.abanet.org/lawyerlocator/searchlawyer.html
This is the address for the ABA's Lawyer Locator service; you can search by area of practice and location.

Lawyers.com
www.lawyers.com
This is the online version of the Martindale-Hubbell directory, the most comprehensive directory of lawyers. You can search by area of practice and location.

FIND A CONTRACTOR

The following national resources provide lists of contractors searchable by city:

Angie's List
www.angieslist.com
Homeowners rate their contractors and describe their experiences. For a fee, you can join and access all the reports filed on your local contractors.

Better Business Bureau
www.bbb.org
This website provides information on businesses; BBB also offers to act as a facilitator between customers and businesses.

National Association of Home Builders
www.nahb.org
The NAHB website provides advice on financing and renovating, as well as a directory of members.

National Association of the Remodeling Industry
www.nari.org
The NARI website provides information on home renovation and a directory of members.

National Kitchen and Bath Association
www.nkba.org
A valuable source of information on kitchen and bath renovation.

FIND AN ARBITRATOR OR MEDIATOR

The groups listed below are major sources for arbitrators and mediators; there are many other sources, including law firms featuring arbitration and mediation services as specialty areas.

American Arbitration Association
www.adr.org
Information on alternative dispute resolution; a source for mediators and arbitrators.

Mediate.com
www.mediate.com
Information on mediation and a source for mediators.

Mediation Works Incorporated
www.mwi.org/index.html
Information on mediation and a source for mediators.

National Arbitration Forum
www.arb-forum.com
A source for information on alternative dispute resolution and
for the names of arbitrators and mediators.

FEDERAL AGENCIES

The Federal Agencies listed below can give you more information about financing your renovation, and avoiding home renovation scams.

Department of Housing and Urban Development
www.hud.gov
Information on government programs to help finance your home
renovation.

Federal Trade Commission
www.ftc.gov
The Federal Trade Commission has a wide range of resources for
consumers, including information about homeowner scams to
avoid.

COMMUNITY ASSOCIATIONS

The groups listed below are good places to start if you are looking for more information about condominiums, cooperatives,
and homeowner associations.

Community Associations Institute
www.caionline.org
Information on homeowner associations, condominiums, and cooperatives.

Uniform Common Interest Ownership Act
www.law.upenn.edu/bll/ulc/fnact99/1990s/ucioa94.htm
This is the legal model for state laws on condominiums, cooperatives, and homeowner associations.

INDEX

accessibility, 4
alteration agreement, 46–47
alternative dispute resolution
  (ADR), 135–45
  arbitration, 141–44
  mediation, 137–41
  small-claims court, 144–45
American Arbitration
  Association (AAA), 143
American Bar Association, xi,
  xiv, 175
annual percentage rate (APR),
  12, 21
appliances, buying for do-it-
  yourself projects, 58–60
appraisals, 11
arbitration, 141–44
  advantages and disadvantages
    of, 144
  arbitrators, 142
  in contract, 108
  cost of, 144
  finding an arbitrator,
    199–200
architects, 6–7
  as mediator, 139
  suing, 149–50
Arizona, complaint procedures
  in, 161–62
asbestos, 121–23
associates, 178
attorney fees. See lawyer fees
attorneys. See lawyers
bait-and-switch, 27, 83,
  169–70
balloon payments, 14, 23
  interest-only balloon loans,
    24–25
bankruptcy of contractor,
  126–27
bathrooms
  do-it-yourself vs. professional
    costs, 5
  recovering costs of, 3
bids, 7, 70–71
blank copies of forms, 21
bonds, 75, 76
  bid bonds, 76
  contract bonds, 77
  contractor's license bonds,
    79–80, 165
  fully insured and bonded,
    76
  payment bonds, 77, 151
  performance bonds, 76–77
  surety bonds, 75–79
books, 188

breach, 96
  dispute resolution and,
    134–35
  suing the contractor, 148
budgeting, 4–5
builder's risk insurance, 75
building codes, 27, 32, 39
building permits, 27, 31–36,
  39
  applying for, 33
  consequences of not
    obtaining, 35–36
  cost of, 34
  determining need for, 6
  do-it-yourself projects, 53,
    57–58
  inspections, 33–35
  inspectors, 35
  online resources, 50–51
  responsibility for, 104–8
  "up to code," 32
business judgment rule, 43–44
California, complaint
  procedures in, 162–63
cash advance checks, 19
cash-out refinancing, 15–16
cash payment, 8–9
CCRs (covenants, conditions,
  and restrictions), 46
change orders, 77, 102
common-interest communities,
  42–49
  condominiums, 44–45, 47
  cooperatives, 45
  governing documents, 46–48
  online resources, 51
  planned unit development,
    48–49
  restrictive covenants, 48–49
  rights to renovate, 6
community associations,
  200–201
community living. See
  common-interest
  communities
Community Reinvestment Act,
  18
complaints, 160, 161–63
  procedures in Arizona,
    161–62
  procedures in California,
    162–63
completion date, 102–3,
  115–16
condominiums, 6, 44–45, 47
construction liens. See
  mechanic's liens

consumer credit, 18
Consumer Fraud Act (New
  Jersey), 167
consumer fraud law, 129–30,
  149, 166–68
consumer protection
  federal, 169–70
  state, 166–68
Consumer Protection Act, 169
contingent-fee arrangements,
  179
contract bonds, 77
contractor bankruptcy, 126–27
contractor estimates, 6–7
contractor financing, 19
contractor license fees, 164
contractor scams, 80–84
contractors, 65–88
  bankruptcy of, 126–27
  bids from, 70–71
  complaints about, 160,
    161–63
  establishing a good
    relationship with, 84–87
  financial stability of, 69
  financing by, 19
  finding, 198–99
  following your instincts, 72
  gathering information about,
    66–67
  handymen vs., 62
  legal history of, 69
  minimizing hassle, 87
  online resources for choosing,
    87–88
  selecting, 66–72
  suing, 148–49
  surety bonds and, 75–79
  unlicensed, 67–68, 75, 161
contractor's home
  improvement loan, 25
contractor's license bonds,
  79–80, 165
contracts, 5, 89–109
  attorney fees and arbitration,
    108
  basics of, 90–91
  breach of, 96, 134–35, 148
  change orders, 102
  changing, 93
  costs, 99–101
  description of work to be
    done, 104
  insurance, 103–4
  lien contracts, 19–20
  lien waivers, 98
  mechanic's liens, 97–98

contracts (*cont.*)
 negotiating, 92–93
 notice to cure, 106
 online resources, 108–9
 oral contracts, 93–95
 payment structure, 101
 permits and inspections, 104–8
 preparation for writing, 91
 responsibility for subcontractors, 105
 review by lawyer, 173
 riders, 93
 right of rescission and, 72
 sample contracts, 197–98
 start date and completion date, 102–3
 warranties, 98–99
 what to include, 96–108
cooperatives, 6, 45
copies of forms, 21
core work, 70
cost-plus basis, 99–100
costs
 additional attorney costs, 180
 of arbitration, 144
 of building permits, 34
 in contract, 99–101
 costs and benefits of renovation, 2–4
 cutting costs, 56, 80
 do-it-yourself projects, 5, 53, 56–57
 recovery of renovation costs, 3
courts of general jurisdiction, 146–47
courts of limited jurisdiction, 146–47
covenants, 48–49
covenants, conditions, and restrictions (CCRs), 46
credit, consumer, 18
credit cards, 19
credit counseling agencies, 18
credit insurance packing, 25–26
credit lines, 15
debt consolidation agencies, 18
debt-to-income ratio, 11
decks, 3
delay, 113–15
depositions, 155, 180
diligence requirement, 103
discovery, 155
discretionary decision, 43–44
dispute resolution, 133–57
 alternative dispute resolution (ADR), 135–45
 lawsuits, 145–56
 negotiating solutions, 133–35
 online resources, 156–57

record keeping, 137
 state licensing boards, 135
do-it-yourself projects, 52–64
 acting as your own general contractor, 54
 before starting, 52–54
 building permits, 53, 57–58
 buying appliances and fixtures, 58–60
 costs, 5, 53, 56–57
 insurance, 53, 57
 online resources, 64
 plans, 54–56
 professional projects *vs.*, 5
 scheduling, 60–61
 subcontractors, 57, 62–64
 variances, 53
document copies, 21
down payments, 101
easements, 38
Environmental Protection Agency, 188
escrow, 21
estimates, 6–7
evaluative mediators, 138
ex parte communications, 141
extended warranties, 59–60
facilitative mediators, 138
factory warranties, 59
failure to complete, 115–16
failure to start, 110–13
false advertising, 169–70
family rooms, recovering renovation costs, 3
Fannie Mae, 16, 17–18
federal agencies, 200
federal consumer protection, 169–70
Federal Home Loan Bank, 18
Federal Housing Administration (FHA), 16–17
Federal Trade Commission, 169–70
fees
 contingent-fee arrangements, 179
 in contract, 108
 contractor license fees, 164
 lawyer fees, 108, 177, 178–82
 of mediators, 140
financial planning, 8
financial stability of contractor, 69
financing, 7–20
 lending law, 20–23
 loans, 10–20
 online resources, 28
 running out of money, 8
 savings and investments, 8–10
 scams, 23–26

financing scams, 23–26
 contractor's home improvement loan, 25
 credit insurance packing, 25–26
 home equity stripping, 24
 interest-only balloon loans, 24–25
 loan flipping, 25
finish work, 70
fixed rate loans, 12
fixtures
 buying for do-it-yourself projects, 58–60
 in rental property, 50
401(k) or 403(b) plans, 9
fraud, 129–31
 consumer fraud law, 129–30, 149, 166–68
 contractor scams, 80–84
 financing scams, 23–26
 Statute of Frauds, 93–94
fully insured and bonded, 76
general contractor, acting as your own, 54
general liability insurance
 for contractors, 73–75, 154
 for do-it-yourself projects, 57
 injuries on the job and, 154
government agencies and legal protections, 158–71
 contractor's license bond, 165
 federal consumer protections, 169–70
 licensing boards, 159–63
 online resources, 170–71
 recovery funds, 163–65
 state and local consumer protection, 166–68
guaranty funds, 163–65
handicap accessibility, 4
handyman *vs.* contractor, 62
hidden problems, 120–26
 asbestos, 121–23
 lead, 123–24
 mold, 124–25
 radon, 125–26
historic districts, 6, 40–41
history of contractor, 69
home equity lines of credit, 15
home equity loans, 14–15
home equity stripping, 24
home improvement loans, 16–17, 25
home office, recovering renovation costs, 3
Home Ownership and Equity Protection Act (HOEPA), 22–23
homeowner loans, 19
homeowner recovery funds, 163–65
homeowners, suing, 151–54

homeowners' associations, 6
homeowner's insurance, 26–28
do-it-yourself projects, 57
escrow and, 21
HomeStyle loans, 17–18
HomeStyle Mortgage, 16
HomeStyle Remodeler loan, 17–18
HUD (U.S. Department of Housing and Urban Development), 187
implied warranty of good workmanship, 71
indemnity provision, 104
injury on the job, 57, 73–75, 154
inspections, 33–35, 104–8
inspectors, 35
insurance, 71, 73–75
builder's risk insurance, 75
in contract, 103–4
credit insurance packing, 25–26
do-it-yourself projects, 53, 57
fully insured and bonded, 76
general liability insurance, 57, 73–75, 154
homeowner's insurance, 21, 26–28, 57
indemnity provision, 104
life insurance loans, 9–10
unlicensed contractors and, 75
waiver of subrogation, 104
workers' compensation insurance, 57, 73–75, 154
interest-only balloon loans, 24–25
interest payments, 8–9
interest rates, 12–14
Internet purchases, 59
investments. See savings and investments
job injuries, 57, 73–75, 154
judgment-proof defendant, 156
kitchens, recovering renovation costs, 3
lawsuits, 145–56
depositions, 155, 180
determining who should be sued, 147–50
discovery phase, 155
how a lawsuit works, 154–56
statutes of limitation, 155
suing the architect, 149–50
suing the contractor, 148–49
suing the homeowner, 151–54
suing the materials supplier, 150

lawyer fees, 178–82
additional costs, 180
in contract, 108
questions about, 177
lawyers, 172–85
comfort level with, 178
contract review by, 173
evaluating, 183–84
finding, 175–76, 198
honesty in dealings with, 184
online resources, 184
questions to ask, 176–78
record keeping, 182
self-representation, 174
when to hire, 172–74
lead paint, 123–24
legal history of contractor, 69
legal protections. See government agencies and legal protections
legal rights and obligations, 5–6
lenders, 21
lending law, 20–23
licenses
contractor license fees, 164
contractor's license bonds, 79–80, 165
unlicensed contractors, 67–68, 75, 161
licensing boards, 159–63
Arizona complaint procedures, 161–62
California complaint procedures, 162–63
Web sites, 191–97
lien contracts, 19–20
lien waivers, 98, 127
lienholder, defined, 97
liens. See also mechanic's liens
defined, 97
notice of lien filing, 152
life insurance loans, 9–10
loan flipping, 25
loans, 10–20
cash-out refinancing, 15–16
consumer credit, 18
contractor financing, 19
credit cards, 19
determining how much you can afford, 11
home equity lines of credit, 15
home equity loans, 14–15
home improvement loans, 16–17
homeowner loans, 19
HomeStyle loans, 17–18
interest rates, 12–14
lien contracts, 19–20
margin loans, 10
redevelopment agencies, 20

unsecured loans, 13–14, 18
value-added mortgages, 16
manufacturer's warranty, 59
margin loans, 10
market value of a home, 11
Martindale-Hubbell Legal Directory, 176
material breach, 96
materials supplier, 169
suing, 150
mechanic's liens, 97–98
contractor bankruptcy and, 127
enforcement, 152–53
notice of lien filing, 152
notice to commence suit, 154
preliminary notice, 152
removing, 153
statutory nature of, 151–52
suing the homeowner, 151–54
mediation, 137–41
architect as mediator, 139
ex parte communications, 141
finding a mediator, 199–200
hiring a mediator, 140
misconduct by contractor or employees, 127–29, 149
misrepresentation, 129–31
mold, 124–25
mycotoxins, 125
National Arbitration Forum (NAF), 143
National Association of Home Builders, 187
National Association of the Remodeling Industry, 186
National Register of Historic Places, 40
negligence, 148–49
negotiation
of contracts, 92–93
in dispute resolution, 133–35
neighbors, 39–40
New Jersey Consumer Fraud Act, 167
notice of lien filing, 152
notice to commence suit, 154
notice to cure, 106
on-the-job injuries, 154
oral contracts, 93–95
overspending, 8
paralegals, 178
parol evidence rule, 94
paying cash, 8–9
payment bonds, 77, 151
payment structure, 101
payments
down payments, 101
interest payments, 8–9
prepayment penalties, 14

performance bonds, 76–77
permits. *See* building permits
personal injury law, 74–75
phasing, 7
plaintiff, 147
planned unit development
　(PUD), 6, 48–49
plans, for do-it-yourself
　projects, 54–56
points, 12
portfolio of securities, 10
preliminary notice, 152
prepayment penalties, 14
process server, 180
property taxes, 21
proprietary leases, 45
punitive damages, 149
radon, 125–26
radon daughters, 126
reasonableness rule, 43
record keeping, 112, 137,
　182
recovery funds, 163–65
recovery of renovation costs, 3
redevelopment agencies, 20
refinancing, 15–16, 21
relationship with contractor,
　84–87
renovation
　costs and benefits of, 2–4
　expenditures for, 1
rental property, 49–50
resale value, 3–4, 7–8
rescission, 21–22, 72
resources, 189
restrictive covenants, 48–49
retirement funds, 9
return on investment, 3
riders, 93
right of rescission, 21–22, 72
rule of reasonableness, 43
running out of money, 8

sample contracts, 197–98
savings and investments,
　8–10
　borrowing against retirement
　　funds, 9
　borrowing from portfolio, 10
　life insurance loans, 9–10
　paying cash, 8–9
scams
　chimney burn scam, 82
　contractor scams, 80–84
　contractor's home
　　improvement loan, 25
　credit insurance packing,
　　25–26
　financing scams, 23–26
　furnace-breaker scam,
　　81–82
　home equity stripping, 24
　interest-only balloon loans,
　　24–25
　leftovers scam, 82
　loan flipping, 25
　warning signs, 83–84
scheduling, for do-it-yourself
　projects, 60–61
second mortgages, 13
secured loans, 13
securities portfolio, 10
security, 13
self-representation, 174
shoddy workmanship, 116–20
small-claims court, 144–45
staging, 7
start date, 102–3
state and local consumer
　protection, 166–68
state licensing boards, 135,
　159–63, 191–97
Statute of Frauds, 93–94
statutes of limitation, 155
statutory damages, 23

subcontractors, 67
　for do-it-yourself projects, 57,
　　62–64
　responsibility for, 105
suing. *See* lawsuits
surety bonds, 75–79
swimming pools, 3
Title I loan, 17
torts, 128
toxic molds, 125
treble damages, 129, 148
Truth in Lending Act (TILA),
　21–22, 169
203(k) loan, 17
unbundling legal services, 182
Uniform Common Interest
　Ownership Act, 44, 45, 51
unlicensed contractors, 67–68,
　75, 161
unsecured loans, 13–14, 18
"up to code," 32
value-added mortgages, 16
variable rate loans, 12
variances, 6, 39, 40, 53
waiver of subrogation, 104
waivers, lien, 98, 127
warranties, 98–99
　in contract, 98–99
　extended warranties, 59–60
　factory warranties, 59
　implied warranty of good
　　workmanship, 71
　manufacturer's warranty, 59
workers' compensation
　insurance, 57, 73–75, 154
workmanship, shoddy, 116–20
zoning, 36–39
　dealing with zoning
　　restrictions, 38
　easements, 38
　how zoning works, 36–38
　quick look at zoning laws, 37

ABOUT THE AUTHOR

Robert Yates is a freelance writer and editor in Evanston, Illinois. He practiced law for ten years before turning to journalism. He was managing editor of the ABA Journal for eight years, and director of the ABA Press for three years. He has also taught journalism at Medill School of Journalism, Northwestern University, and Dominican University.

ABOUT THE AUTHOR

Robert Yates is a freelance writer and editor in Evanston, Illinois. He practiced law for ten years before turning to journalism. He was managing editor of the ABA Journal for eight years, and director of the ABA Press for three years. He has also taught journalism at Medill School of Journalism, Northwestern University, and Dominican University.